AF616034

Photo by Mark Morelli

A scene from the Trinity Repertory Company production of "Mrs. Sedgewick's Head." Set design by Eugene Lee.

MRS. SEDGEWICK'S HEAD

BY TOM GRIFFIN

★

★

DRAMATISTS
PLAY SERVICE
INC.

SPECIAL NOTE

Anyone receiving permission to produce MRS. SEDGEWICK'S HEAD is required (1) to give credit to the Author as sole and exclusive Author of the Play on the title page of all programs distributed in connection with performances of the Play and in all instances in which the title of the Play appears for purposes of advertising, publicizing or otherwise exploiting the Play and/or a production thereof. The name of the Author must appear on a separate line, in which no other name appears, immediately beneath the title and in size of type equal to 50% of the size of the largest, most prominent letter used for the title of the Play. No person, firm or entity may receive credit larger or more prominent than that accorded the Author; and (2) to give the following acknowledgment on the title page in all programs distributed in connection with performances of the Play:

World Premiere Presented at
Trinity Repertory Company Theatre

Richard Jenkins — Artistic Director
Dennis Conway — General Manager

September, 1993

SPECIAL NOTE ON SONGS AND RECORDINGS

For performance of the songs, arrangements, recordings and photographs mentioned in this Play that are protected by copyright, the permission of the copyright owners must be obtained; or other songs and recordings in the public domain substituted.

MRS. SEDGEWICK'S HEAD received its premiere at Trinity Repertory Company (Richard Jenkins, Artistic Director; Dennis Conway, General Manager) in Providence, Rhode Island, on September 21, 1993. It was directed by David Wheeler; the set and lighting designs were by Eugene Lee; the costume design was by William Lane; the sound design was by Benjamin Emerson; and the stage manager was Bonnie J. Baggesen. The cast was as follows:

NATE BECK .... Joseph Hindy
LINCOLN ANDRICH .... Jonathan Fried
BENJAMIN .... Christopher Byrnes
ROBERT CAHILL .... Richard Kneeland
JOHNNY SIMMONS .... Timothy Crowe
LINDSAY MCCALL .... Nance Williamson
ARTHUR WINTER .... William Damkoehler
CARA .... Cynthia Strickland
EDDIE STOPANOKOVITCH .... Robert J. Colonna
RON SIMMONS .... Dan Welch

CHARACTERS

NATE BECK
LINCOLN ANDRICH
BENJAMIN
ROBERT CAHILL
JOHNNY SIMMONS
LINDSAY MCCALL
ARTHUR WINTER
CARA
EDDIE STOPANOKOVITCH
RON SIMMONS

TIME

The present. And an October day five years ago.

PLACE

Los Angeles. And a small rustic community in upstate New York.

SETTING

The play is divided into scenes which take place in a variety of settings. These should vary from minimal to suggestive to, in the case of Johnny's house, somewhat realistic. There are also numerous opportunities in the script for the use of slides and/or film. Although not necessary, they serve several purposes, not the least of which is to provide a visual counterpoint to the subject of the play itself. The fluidity of scenes is essential. Ideally the only blackouts should be those specifically indicated in the script.

MRS. SEDGEWICK'S HEAD

ACT ONE

From the darkness, there are the insistent strains of LA restaurant Musak. Cheerful and dull. The lights bump up surprisingly on a restaurant that takes itself too seriously.*

Nate Beck, an aggressive film producer, sits with Lincoln Andrich, an ostensibly benign young studio executive wearing a good suit. They are working on some drinks, studying their menus.

LINCOLN. I've never ... eaten here. You know, only drinks and things.
NATE. Try the mako. They do a little butter, a little herb, grill the thing. It's nice.
LINCOLN. Shark? I don't think so.
NATE. Hey, Lincoln, it was a movie. A Spielberg movie.
LINCOLN. But ... shark.
NATE. So? You think every shark gets its protein from dead teenagers? C'mon. Lighten up.
LINCOLN. I'll have the luncheon steak. It's safer.
NATE. Safer? Kid, this is Hollywood. The flash and dash capital of the universe. Safe doesn't do it here. Meat and potatoes on Sunset? *Nolo contendre,* baby. *(Signals the waiter.)* Benjamin! *(Benjamin enters. A properly obsequious Hollywood waiter.)*
BENJAMIN. Mr. Beck. Ready to order?
NATE. Benjamin, Mr. Andrich here is an executive over at Golden Mirror Studios. He's a comer. But he's a little cautious about the mako. So is the mako delicious or is the mako delicious?
BENJAMIN. The mako is pretty ... delicious. It flakes much

* See Special Note on Songs and Recordings on copyright page.

nicer than you'd expect from a ... you know, carnivore.
NATE. Carnivore? Don't scare the kid. It's a fish. A mako is just a fish with teeth! Jesus!
BENJAMIN. I didn't mean carnivore in the sense of ... carnivore ...
NATE. No? Well, how many ways can a guy mean "carnivore"?
BENJAMIN. I don't follow.
NATE. How many meanings does "carnivore" have?
BENJAMIN. *(Boggled.)* How many?
NATE. How many?
BENJAMIN. I don't know.
NATE. One. A fucking meateater. That's it. That's the range of its definitional potential. And you use it to try to convince Mr. Andrich not be concerned with ordering the mako? Jesus ...
LINCOLN. I'll try it. I'll have the carni ... the mako.
BENJAMIN. An excellent choice, sir.
NATE. Let me have the luncheon sirloin with a side order of steamed asparagus. Steamed. Not soggy. And maybe a salad. Lincoln, you want a salad? Octopus salad? You ever try octopus salad?
LINCOLN. No. I've had snail salad. It isn't very ...
NATE. Snails! Yuck! You know how those goddamn things live?! It's unbelievable. They crawl all day long. They should be screenwriters, huh? *(All three break into laughter.)*
LINCOLN. I'll try the octopus.
BENJAMIN. Two octopus salads.
NATE. No, not for me. I don't eat things that swim under rocks at four thousand pounds per square inch. I'm afraid the things'll explode in my stomach nine hours later. No thank you. Let me have a small dinner salad. French dressing's fine. But not that sewerage out of the bottle. House French.
BENJAMIN. House French it is, Mr. Beck. *(Benjamin exits. Nate looks around. A conspiratorial pause.)*
NATE. You know how I get this table? This very conspicuous well-placed table? I overtip everybody. The *maitre d'.* The busboys. The waiters. The cokeheads who park the Jag. The

ninety-three year old pervert who hands out towels in the men's room. Everybody. Christ, one time I tipped a customer. Really. The guy was so overdressed, I thought he was the wine steward! *(A breath.)* So Artie couldn't make it. Hey, no, I understand. The Head of Motion Pictures. A lot of responsibilities. You ever go golfing with Artie?

LINCOLN. No. I haven't been with Golden Mirror long. I actually don't ... socialize with Mr. Winter.

NATE. He's a horrendous golfer. Terrible sport. Moans and groans his way around the course. He hits a bad shot, you'd think CBS was hiding in the bushes with a mini-cam. We did the Pro/Am together out at Pebble Beach. You know who Artie got teamed up with? Gary Player. Unbelievable. You know who I got? Tony Orlando. Nice guy, but as a golfer he's a singer. *(A moment.)* So what do you do over there? Man the copier, chaperone the starlets, what?

LINCOLN. Development.

NATE. Development? What the fuck is development, anyway?

LINCOLN. You know, search for projects, try to marry the proper elements ...

NATE. *(With an edge.)* Hey, Lincoln, I been in this racket now for over twenty years. I know what development is. Okay?

LINCOLN. Sure. Okay.

NATE. But tell me the truth, you development guys, you ever get laid? I mean, importantly laid? Not some D-girl laid, but high profile laid? A chick with her name above the title laid? No way. You think Cher knows what development is? She thinks it's something you do with your goddamn deltoids. *(Thinks about this.)* What is a deltoid, anyway?

LINCOLN. The ... back? I'm not sure. Mr. Winter asked me to discuss ...

NATE. Ahh, so it's cut the gratuitous chatter time, huh? I like that.

LINCOLN. I apologize if I seemed ...

NATE. Hey, Lincoln, cut the shit. You said The Studio had some stuff they wanted to run by me. We're doing lunch here at Chez Bring-Your-Gold-Card. Fine. I'm a big boy. I've produced sixteen films. I've met Siskel and Ebert both. One's fat.

The other's skinny. I've been at enough benefits I can identify every LA caterer who ever touched a goddamn radish. I'm a grownup in The Land of Make Believe. Give it to me.
LINCOLN. The Studio, Mr. Winter actually ... thinks the book is terrific. Viable and accessible and commercial. And your acquisition of the option is a tribute to your vision.
NATE. Great. You love the book. Good. But there's a hitch, right?
LINCOLN. There's always a hitch, Mr. Beck.
NATE. Nate.
LINCOLN. Nate.
NATE. You guys hate the title, right? *Mrs. Sedgewick's Head.* I agree. It sucks. Literary and oblique and "Who the Hell Knows What Kind of a Picture This Is Anyway?" I agree. Of course, that's what Dedalus calls the novel.
LINCOLN. The title is fine.
NATE. *(A little off-balance.)* Oh? It is? Well, great. So what's the hitch? Let me guess. Artie doesn't like the idea of Andy Castleman directing. That's fine. It was just an idea. Did you see his last film?
LINCOLN. It cost twenty-three million. The Studio pulled it in three weeks. They couldn't give the foreign rights away.
NATE. I'm not surprised. Artsy-craftsy piece of shit. I mean, who does a movie starring two unknowns: one a kid named Lance with a speech impediment; the other, a flat-chested girl who speaks like she played the banjo in *Deliverance? (Benjamin reappears. He serves each of the men a rather elaborate looking salad. Nate studies it as if it were hospital waste.)*
BENJAMIN. Enjoy, gentlemen.
NATE. What is this?
BENJAMIN. The octopus salad, Mr. Beck.
NATE. I didn't order the octopus salad. I ordered a dinner salad with House French. Am I losing my mind here? Lincoln, did I order the octopus salad?
BENJAMIN. I'm sorry, sir. My mist ...
NATE. No, let him answer. I want some confirmation on this.
LINCOLN. I think the dinner salad.
BENJAMIN. It's no problem, Mr. Beck. My apologies. I'll just

take it back. You'll have your dinner salad pronto.

NATE. I don't mean to be a prick here, Benjy, but what's going on that you bring me octopus salad when I've been coming here for maybe four years now and never once have I ordered the goddamn thing? Never. I hate octopus. Tentacles. Suckers. Those big goony eyes like in the cartoons. The very thought of it makes ...

LINCOLN. Nate.... It's just a mistake.

BENJAMIN. I'm really very sorry.

NATE. No. No. I'm overreacting. You're right. Fine. Just bring me the dinner salad. House French. House. *(Benjamin exits, a bit ruffled.)* Do you believe this? You'd think I was some guy in a Banlon shirt from Iowa or somewhere. Some guy who's biggest thrill in life is taking a phony Beverly Hills bus tour where they point out Guccis and, "On your right is the gracious home of Ricardo Montalban." Jesus. *(Recovering.)* Go on. Eat. It's.... Go on. You'll like it.

LINCOLN. *(Taking a bite.)* It's ... okay ...

NATE. *(Cannot let it go.)* Of course, it's no fucking wonder. You should see the kitchen. The place is crawling with ... I don't know what they are. Indonesians or something. Bunch of sinister looking guys with funny scarves acting like they all slept with Julia Child last night. America, huh? *(A pause. Lincoln pecks at his salad, then suddenly stops and assesses Nate. The ingenuous assistant seems to be vanishing.)*

LINCOLN. The Studio thinks it's premature to go with a director. We want a strong screenplay, then we'll have a better sense of things.

NATE. Sure. No, I can appreciate that. So we need a writer, right? No problem. *(Actually producing a list.)* I got an A List. I got a B List.

LINCOLN. Mr. Winter's not interested in lists.

NATE. Hey, these are quality writers. We're not talking hacks here.

LINCOLN. *(Sharply, factually.)* Mr. Winter has already chosen the writer.

NATE. *(Clearly astounded.)* Huh?

LINCOLN. He doesn't care to be involved with the project

unless we're allowed to select the writer. And he's picked the writer. *(A nervous Benjamin reappears with the dinner salad. He places it down. Nate doesn't seem to notice.)*

BENJAMIN. Again, my apologies, Mr. Beck. Will there be anything else?

NATE. Huh? No. Nothing. Thanks. *(Benjamin exits.)* Who?

LINCOLN. Who what?

NATE. You know who what. Don't get cute, Lincoln. Who does Artie have in mind?

LINCOLN. Johnny Simmons.

NATE. *(Practically gasping.)* Johnny ...!! Johnny Simmons!? You're kidding me, right? I mean, this is some sick joke, right? Some goddamn industry prank, am I correct on this?

LINCOLN. No joke. Mr. Winter has given it considerable thought. He feels Johnny Simmons is a natural for this project.

NATE. A natural for ... Johnny Simmons is a goddamn basket case. He's got burnout so bad his burnout has burnout. Johnny Simmons! Are you people fucking nuts! The sonovabitch lives in a cave somewhere! He's so "sensitive", he has to be medicated to watch *Mr. Ed!* Johnny Simmons.... This is unbelievable ...

LINCOLN. I'm sorry, Mr. Beck, but that's what The Studio wants.

NATE. Oh, yeah?! Well, you can tell The Studio to go fuck itself! I'll go someplace else. I don't need to take this autocratic garbage. The whole town'll be scrambling to get a piece of this thing.

LINCOLN. *(Utter coldness.)* Who?

NATE. Whaddya mean, "Who?"

LINCOLN. Who'll be doing the scrambling?

NATE. What? You think Golden Mirror is the only game in town? C'mon, Lincoln, smell the celluloid. Just because you guys have two or three hot pictures, all of a sudden you think you're some kind of Century City gurus? Bullshit! *(Just occurs to him.)* Where'd you go to school?

LINCOLN. School? Yale.

NATE. Yale. Big fucking deal. I've been to Yale. You know what Yale is? A bunch of precious rich kids surrounded by a slum. You ever leave the campus? You ever see what's around you?

LINCOLN. There's no reason to be insulting, Mr. Beck.

NATE. Yale ... Jesus. Perfect. You know where I went to school?

LINCOLN. This really isn't necessary.

NATE. Where do you think?

LINCOLN. I ... I really don't have any ...

NATE. Guess.

LINCOLN. I can't.

NATE. Harvard. That's right, Lincoln. Harvard. "Park your car in the Harvard yard." That Harvard. B.A., M.B.A., M.O.U.S.E.! Christ, I had Nobel laureates teaching me Biology I. My freshman roommate was a Hungarian prince. Honest to God. Decadent drone of a kid named Gulag or something, but a legitimate prince! You think because I'm this crass loud sonovabitch, it's impossible I could've ever had an education, right? Admit it.

LINCOLN. Frankly, the whole issue never occurred to me.

NATE. I've read, are you ready for this?, fucking Shakespeare in French. That's Harvard. That explains it all. They take English speaking kids and they make them read French translations of English literature. And this they call Higher Education! *(On a roll.)* I had a professor in Tax Law. Name of Krupky or Rupky or something. A real genius. He used to get audited about once a week. He couldn't do his own short form on a bet. Tax professor, my ass! Higher education! Harvard! Please! *(Lincoln listens with a certain grim fascination as Nate continues.)* Artie wants Johnny Simmons because Johnny Simmons'll create press. That's why. Bottom line. Johnny Simmons is a nut case and *People* magazine'll come out with some goddamn special issue or something: "Johnny's Back!"

LINCOLN. Johnny Simmons had three Oscar nominations in five years.

NATE. Johnny Simmons killed his brother in a cherry orchard in upstate New York! He shot him in the head, covered his body with a Winnie the Pooh comforter, called the cops, and sat over the still warm corpse reading excerpts from his own fucking stuff! *(A breath.)* Johnny Simmons is a homicidal maniac.

LINCOLN. It was a mercy killing.

NATE. Oh, really? Then how come he spent four and a half years in prison?

LINCOLN. *(Tiring of this.)* The point is, Mr. Winter wants him. If you want our involvement on *Mrs. Sedgewick's Head,* you get Johnny Simmons.

NATE. And if I don't?

LINCOLN. Go someplace else.

NATE. You're a cute one, Lincoln. *(Imitating him.)* "Oh, horrors, octopus! Oh, what a fancy restaurant! Oh, Mr. Winter is such a nice man!" And beneath it all, you're just this slimebucket like the rest of us. You're a beaut.

LINCOLN. *(Quietly vicious.)* Really? Well, now it's my turn, Mr. Beck. You can't go anyplace else and you know it. You've exhausted your contacts. You haven't had a moneymaker in over six years. You've offended just about everybody in this town. Your name comes up and sophisticated men groan. How you ever got your hands on this novel I'll never know, but we want the project. And we want Johnny Simmons. And we expect you to do the pitch. And do you know why? Because Mr. Winter thinks you have a terrific chance with him because Simmons'll find you ... amusing. Idiosyncratic. Like some Sammy Glick prototype that managed to escape the evolutionary scheme. That's why. Take it or leave it. *(Silence. Nate reacts as if he'd been wounded. He takes a huge swallow from his drink. Weak.)*

NATE. Jesus ...

LINCOLN. And one final thing. One final piece of the puzzle that you might find provocative.

NATE. And what would that be?

LINCOLN. Did it ever occur to you that Stephen Dedalus, the author of *Mrs. Sedgewick's Head,* was a pseudonym? Did it ever cross your supposedly well-educated mind that Stephen Dedalus was the hero of James Joyce's *Portrait of the Artist As a Young Man?* Harvard my ass. Did you ever meet the author, ever talk with him?

NATE. No, I ... Who cares about a novelist. I just met with the agent. Some dinosaur named Cahill who ...
LINCOLN. *(Cutting through.)* Johnny Simmons wrote the book, Mr. Beck. Johnny Simmons wrote *Mrs. Sedgewick's Head.* Johnny Simmons is Stephen Dedalus. He conceived it in prison. He memorized it. And when he got out, he sat down and wrote it all down. Word for word. Like some kind of deranged superhuman computer. And that's why we want him. Period. *(Nate is awestruck. He looks around him as if unsure of his environment. Benjamin enters. He brings two plates: one with the mako, the other with the luncheon sirloin.)*
BENJAMIN. *(Serving Lincoln.)* The sirloin. *(Serving Nate.)* And the grilled mako. *(Starts to leave.)* Gentlemen, enjoy.
NATE. *(Stunned.)* This is the shark. You gave me the shark.
BENJAMIN. Yes. Uh huh?
NATE. He ordered the shark. I didn't order the shark. He did.
BENJAMIN. *(Starting to rearrange.)* I'm sorry, Mr. Beck. This really isn't one of my better days.
NATE. And my asparagus. My steamed asparagus. Where the hell is it?
LINCOLN. We'll just switch the plates. It's fine.
NATE. To you it's fine! To me it's crap! I mean, first the octopus, now the shark! What do I look like? A tourist?! Some goddamn chronic Midwestern fish-eater!!
BENJAMIN. I'm sorry, Mr. Beck. Really. I just transposed the ...
NATE. Transposed? Well, transpose this: I wouldn't eat shark if I were stranded in a Burger King. You hear me? Do you know what they eat? People! Goddamn people! They're ... carnivores!!
LINCOLN. I'll just take the shark.
NATE. *(To Benjamin, very close.)* Did you see *Jaws?* Huh? Did you see it?
BENJAMIN. Really, Mr. Beck ...
LINCOLN. Nate ...
NATE. You shut the fuck up! *(To Benjamin, relentless.)* Did you or did you not see the movie, *Jaws?*

BENJAMIN. *(Very flustered.)* Yes.

NATE. What did the shark in *Jaws* eat?

BENJAMIN. People?

NATE. What kind of people?

BENJAMIN. Tourists? White people? I don't know ...

LINCOLN. Nate, this really isn't ...

NATE. What kind of white people? Old white people? Middle aged white people? Baby white people?

BENJAMIN. *(As if a contestant.)* Teenagers...?!

NATE. Exactly! Bingo! Teenagers! Need we fucking say more! Sharks eat teenagers!! Roll the credits!!! *(The lights quickly fade on Nate and Lincoln as the credits for this particular stage production begin to roll:* "Mrs. Sedgewick's Head *by Tom Griffin. Directed by ..." Etcetera. This is accompanied by overly dramatic 40s movie credit music.* As the credits end, the lights bump up on Robert Cahill, a distinguished looking man in late middle age. He wears an impeccable suit. He looks to the audience, as if suddenly aware of their presence.)*

CAHILL. *(To the audience.)* I've been a New York literary agent since the first hairy mastodon bought his first hairy typewriter. The joke here in the halls of Thompkins & Storch is that my client list once included Plutarch, Euripides, and a very talkative young Homer. Most of this is just nonsense. I never even knew Euripides. *(Amused by his own joke.)* When Johnny Simmons came out of prison, he called and asked if I'd represent him. Seeing as how I'd never met the man and knew he'd had prominent agents on both coasts, I was quite shocked. I suggested we meet. "It's not necessary, Mr. Cahill," he said. "I'll send you my new book. You sell it. You take your ten percent. Send me the rest." I was intrigued. I insisted on a meeting. He finally acquiesced. *(A bewildered smile.)* Johnny, you must understand, has a knack, a flair really, for the peculiar. We met in an abandoned boathouse in upstate New York. Ichabod Crane country. Dark. Full of headless ghosts. *(A nocturnal bird screeches as Cahill moves to another area of the stage. A poorly lit shack with eerie splintered light angling in from above.*

* See Special Note on Songs and Recordings on copyright page.

Cahill stands, clearly uncomfortable. He holds a manuscript box. Sitting across from him, obscured by shadows, is Johnny Simmons. A man in his forties, he wears gray workclothes.) When you said we'd meet in the middle of nowhere, I thought you were exaggerating. Not so, Mr. Simmons. *(Nothing.)* Not so.... Indeed ... *(Indicating the manuscript.)* I'm anxious to read it. You say you memorized it in prison, memorized it and then typed it up once you got out?

JOHNNY. Yes.

CAHILL. That's quite a feat. How much revising did you do?

JOHNNY. None.

CAHILL. Oh ... *(Silence. Unnerved, Cahill looks around him at the boathouse.)* The thing about the name. The Stephen Dedalus. People will know, of course, that it's a pseudonym. There still are educated people in the world. *(Nothing.)* It'll get out. I mean, no matter how diligent one is, there's always a leak. And, despite your reluctance, Mr. Simmons, anonymity won't come easily. *(Johnny remains still. Cahill is getting anxious.)* There's also the business about film rights. Admittedly, I haven't yet read the book, but assuming it's of your usual quality, there will be attempts to secure the rights. Options. That sort of thing. Hollywood folks can be very aggressive. *(A self-conscious laugh.)* But I suppose you know all about these machinations. *(As if suddenly reminded, Johnny looks down at his legs, then to Cahill, almost accusingly.)*

JOHNNY. People talk about my leg. They see the limp. They see me dragging it around like some ... vestigial organ. They talk.

CAHILL. Pardon?

JOHNNY. All the tendons and muscles in my left ankle were severed.

CAHILL. Severed? By what? *(Suddenly, Johnny stops. It is as if the memory has faded. He gives Cahill a sharp look; then, all business, reels off his instructions.)*

JOHNNY. Sell the book for the first offer over a million. No auction. Just a straight-up sale. Negotiate the percentages. Do the boiler plate and the subsidiaries up front with the following conditions: give the film option to the first credible producer to come up with two hundred and fifty grand for six months. Two hundred and fifty against two-point-five million. One time renewable. Juggle the points if you have to. Don't waste time doing lunch and returning calls. God speed.

CAHILL. "God speed," to be sure. Two-point-five million for an unpublished pseudonymous novel.... And why me, Mr. Simmons? You've had exceptional representation for many years.

JOHNNY. Those relationships were terminated during my incarceration. *(An alarming smile.)* You've a reputation for integrity. You'll do your job. *(Johnny extends a hand. Bewildered, Cahill shakes it. Johnny starts away.)*

CAHILL. That's it? *(Johnny limps toward the door.)* What makes you think anybody'll pay this kind of money? Nobody's even read the novel! *(Johnny stops and turns. He smiles. Not without a trace of madness.)*

JOHNNY. I'm a freak, Mr. Cahill. This is America. Freaks sell. *(Johnny exits. Cahill steps forward.)*

CAHILL. *(To the audience.)* I sold the book in three days. I negotiated the film option in eight. A coarse resourceful man named Nathaniel Beck. He thought Stephen Dedalus was the author's actual name. *(Sighs, laughs.)* Hollywood. Alas! Hollywood. *(A contemporary romantic ballad* bumps up as the lights crossfade from the boathouse to Lindsay McCall's office. A desk stacked with manuscripts. A substantial decorator-chosen painting. As LA as it gets. Lindsay sits on the floor, doing some stretching exercises. Maybe thirty, she is strikingly good looking. Bright, stylish, ambitious. Decked out in snazzy exercise gear and barefoot, she wiggles her toes, studying them as if they belonged to some other body. There is a quick knock on the door, followed by the entrance of Arthur Winter. He is the Head of Motion Pictures at an up and coming studio and looks it. He is confident, smart, and a very young fifty-five.)*

ARTHUR. Hi, Lindsay McCall.

LINDSAY. Hi, Arthur Winter.

ARTHUR. Whatcha doing?

LINDSAY. Hating my feet.

ARTHUR. Good activity. The plane was late. I sat next to a

* See Special Note on Songs and Recordings on copyright page.

man who claimed he flew first class so that when the plane went down, he'd die first. I passed on the veal piccata.

LINDSAY. So how's New York?

ARTHUR. Great. Parts of it actually resemble The United States.

LINDSAY. And how were the captains of industry?

ARTHUR. Oh, the usual. They had the meeting at a Swiss restaurant. Me and the board of directors sitting around trying to figure out what "A Vodka Slalom" was.

LINDSAY. I didn't know the Swiss had restaurants.

ARTHUR. Restaurants, yes. Food, no. How did things go with Lincoln and Nate Beck?

LINDSAY. Fair. I gather Nate was sort of a cross between Aristotle Onassis and Lou Costello. Oh, and Lincoln also reported that Nate threatened to kill him in the parking lot.

ARTHUR. And?

LINDSAY. And he didn't.

ARTHUR. Nate'll come around.

LINDSAY. I'm always surprised he knows how to use silverware.

ARTHUR. He's a film producer. What do you expect? David Niven?

LINDSAY. You think it's smart to let him anywhere near Johnny Simmons? Nate Beck and Lincoln Andrich meeting with this legendary ... murderer cum novelist cum screenwriter? It sounds ...

ARTHUR. Lincoln? Who said anything about Lincoln?

LINDSAY. You let him deal with Nate.

ARTHUR. Nate's one thing. Johnny Simmons is another. He'd eat Lincoln alive. Lincoln's an arrogant kid. A smart aleck careerist.

LINDSAY. You're going to send Nate alone?

ARTHUR. No. This is too delicate for that. If Simmons says no to doing the screenplay, the whole project collapses. *(A calculated pause.)* I'm sending you with him.

LINDSAY. Me?

ARTHUR. You. Aren't you curious about the notorious Mr. Simmons?

LINDSAY. Sure. But being with Nate Beck for more than two minutes gives me the chills. The man should be chained to Jane Goodall. *(A moment.)* What's Simmons like?

ARTHUR. Dangerously intelligent. Insidious.

LINDSAY. What's that mean?

ARTHUR. When Johnny was hot, which was often, he played the game as well as anybody. He always managed to be overpaid, over-indulged, and over-negotiated. And now he's a celebrated schizophrenic with a prison record, a murdered brother, a hot property, and more guile than a Bel Air concierge. *(An honest warning.)* Watch your step, Lindsay. Or he'll devour you. *(Arthur exits. Lindsay comes forward.)*

LINDSAY. *(To the audience.)* My official title here at Golden Mirror is Vice President in Charge of Creative Affairs. My job is full of perks. And random uglinesses. I spent yesterday arguing with a post-pubescent film star. The boy, proclaiming he's sensitive to "the needs of the extras", had demanded CD players in the Port-O-Johns. You've heard of bad hair days. This jerk was having a bad cerebral cortex day. Arthur Winter, my boss, is a well-mannered megalomaniacal sexist, but I like him. It's hard to know whether he's sending me as negotiator with Simmons or babysitter for Beck. Probably a bit of both. After years of fending off venal Hollywood flesh monsters, I figure Johnny Simmons will be a piece of cake. After the LA snakepit, how tough can a guy be who lives in a cabin in the woods? *(Starts to leave.)* P.S. If Nate Beck tries to lay a finger on me, I plan on castrating the man. With manicure scissors probably. *(A smile.)* See, I told you there were perks. *(The lights quickly crossfade to Johnny's kitchen. Dominated by a large oak table, the room exudes rusticity. Cara is busy sorting through a stack of mail. She is a woman in her forties. Plainly dressed, she possesses a keen, but unpracticed, intelligence. Eddie enters from outside. He is a good natured soul of indeterminate age who lives with an easy grin and a bad wardrobe. He carries several tabloid newspapers and a toolbox with "Eddie" boldly hand-emblazoned on its side. Cara opens an envelope and studies its contents. Absorbed.)*

EDDIE. You should see it outside. Jeepers! It's gloomier than a priest's wallet.

CARA. What?
EDDIE. "Gloomier than a priest's wallet." Just a common phrase. *(Eddie pours himself coffee, sits, and starts to read a tabloid.)*
CARA. The film people are coming in three days. They plan to stay for only a few hours. Then they're flying back out. Their intention is to convince Johnny to write the screenplay. *(An ironic laugh.)* I told Cahill it was a waste of time. He said they "demanded" it. "Contractual niceties were in order." You know what Johnny said? "I'd love to meet them, Cara. Have them fax me a collective persona." *(Sadly.)* They have no idea …
EDDIE. *(Obliviously reading.)* Yup. Jeepers! The old barometer's dropping like a banker's heart.
CARA. Where do you pick up these common phrases, Eddie?
EDDIE. Around. *(Looks upstairs.)* So where is the genius today?
CARA. In his garret. Where else?
EDDIE. He sure is a secrete-ive one.
CARA. Secret-ive.
EDDIE. That's what I said.
CARA. No. You said, "Secrete-ive." Secrete-ive means he's oozing something. Secret-ive means he's hiding something.
EDDIE. Oh. *(A thoughtful moment.)* Jeepers! So what if you were hiding ooze?
CARA. What?
EDDIE. Would you be secret-ive or secrete-ive?
CARA. Who'd hide ooze?
EDDIE. I dunno. Somebody ashamed of it, I guess.
CARA. Eddie, your brain should be stored in a Kryptonite jar. You know, for future generations to study at their leisure.
EDDIE. *(As if it just hit him.)* These film people, do they … understand about Johnny?
CARA. No.
EDDIE. I mean, do they expect to find some guy they can … I don't know, communicate with?
CARA. Probably.
EDDIE. So why doesn't somebody tell 'em?
CARA. Tell them what?
EDDIE. I don't know. That Johnny's carburetor is full of water maybe?

CARA. What?

EDDIE. You know what I mean, Cara. That Johnny's Green Stamps have lost their glue. That his toaster doesn't pop.

CARA. You're an amazing man, Eddie Stopanokovitch.

EDDIE. Shouldn't somebody just tell 'em?

CARA. They insisted on a meeting. So they'll get a meeting.

EDDIE. Yeah. With a guy whose weed whacker has run out of string. *(Eddie blithely returns to his reading. Cara comes forward.)*

CARA. *(To the audience.)* When Johnny got out of prison, he asked if I'd be his secretary. We'd known each other forever. Long before his Rich and Famous stage. I said yes. And so here I am. Ex-waitress. Two time divorcee. High school graduate. Executive secretary. Chef. Girl Friday. Only friend. *(A lamentable fact.)* Johnny is crazy and sad. I think of leaving every day. But I don't. *(Beginning to leave.)* He doesn't often speak about that night. About killing Ron. About how it came to pass. It was a raw October day. Ron had showed up unexpectedly on the doorstep of this very house around noon. He was cold. And hungry. And dying. *(Cara exits. As does Eddie. It is the past. The main room is quickly bathed in a stark October light. Johnny is motionless as he listens to Ron, his younger brother. Ron is a man in his thirties. He wears work clothes. Despite an ostensible averageness, he is on the edge of the edge.)*

RON. I'm so scared, Johnny. All the time. I mean, when the doctor first said, "Leukemia," I got the first rush of it. The fear. Like this jolt of it. I tried to stand up and ... I fell! Collapsed! The doctor said it happens that way sometimes. I was so ... embarrassed, Johnny. I just got this death sentence from this stranger and all I could think about was what a pathetic thing I must look like lying on the floor. What a cowardly pathetic excuse for ... *(Looks around.)* You got any food?

JOHNNY. Sure. What do you want?

RON. They said I'd lose my appetite, but, you know, it hasn't happened that way. I'm still hungry a lot, but.... But I throw up all the time. I always hated that. Throwing up. Remember how I hated that?

JOHNNY. I remember.

RON. I'm cold. I'm always cold.

JOHNNY. I'll give the heat a boost ...

RON. *(A sudden violent wail.)* It's from inside, Johnny! I'm cold inside!! *(Very shaken, Ron goes to his coat and gets a small package. He presents it to Johnny.)*

JOHNNY. What's this?

RON. Open it.

JOHNNY. Can't it wait?

RON. Open it. *(Johnny opens the package. He reaches inside and pulls out a pistol. For a long moment, he just studies it, unnerved.)*

JOHNNY. Where'd you get this?

RON. The gun store. Where else? *(Thinks about this.)* It's easier to buy a gun than it is to cash a check. Really. You ever try to cash a check at one of those big discount stores? It's like torture. Credit torture. *(Long pause.)* I can't live with this any more, older brother. I don't have any family. My ex-wife is remarried. I sold my landscaping business. I told you that, right?

JOHNNY. Right.

RON. It wasn't much of a business, but, you know, goodwill, tools, the truck, all that shit. It adds up.

JOHNNY. *(Dully.)* I'm sure.

RON. I don't want to be one of those guys who leaves all the pieces to be sorted out. I don't want to be a goddamn burden in death. So everything's in order.

JOHNNY. In order for what?

RON. I can't do it myself, Johnny. Honest, I've tried. But I can't. I hold the gun. I start to pull the trigger. But ... I just get paralyzed. I can't do it myself.

JOHNNY. You're not suggesting...?

RON. Yeah. Yeah, I am.

JOHNNY. I couldn't do that, Ron.

RON. You could.

JOHNNY. I couldn't!

RON. Oh, you could, Johnny. I know you could. I even know where. The cherry orchard. You know, where we used to go play. It'd, and I know this sounds macabre and all, but it'd be a great place to die. I mean, you're the writer. "Great," is a lousy word. What would be the word?

JOHNNY. I ... don't ...

RON. *(Suddenly wild again.)* You're the writer! You come up with the word! It'd be a blank-blank place to die! You're the writer!!

JOHNNY. Jesus ... *(Pause.)* Poetic?

RON. I'm so goddamn hungry all the time. I think maybe it's from all the throwing up. You think it's because of that?

JOHNNY. Maybe. I don't ...

RON. "Poetic." That's nice. It'd be a real poetic place to die. The cherry orchard. *(Laughs.)* Remember how when you came back from college, we went out there one day and you said, "It reminds me of Chekhov." And I said, "The guy on *Star Trek?*" And you laughed at me. And I got pissed and you got pissed and one thing led to another and we didn't even speak for like weeks? Remember that?

JOHNNY. Well, it was a stupid observation.

RON. *(Legitimately irritated.)* Why? Because you're so fucking educated and I'm the nitwit younger brother.

JOHNNY. Something like that.

RON. Because I didn't know about some fucking dead fucking Russian fucking playwright!

JOHNNY. It was Chekhov for Christ's sake!

RON. Hey, Johnny, who the fuck cares!

JOHNNY. I care! Anton Fucking Chekhov!!

RON. So the Chekov in *Star Trek?* He don't count?

JOHNNY. That's right. "He don't count."

RON. Then how come, Mr. Pretentious Overeducated Asshole, that more people in the world know about the guy on *Star Trek* who "don't count" than know about this Russian who lived a million years ago and nobody can stay awake through his goddamn plays anyway!!

JOHNNY. Perfect. That's like saying how come more people have heard of Salvador Dali than Rene Magritte! *(Ron cannot believe this arcane observation. He makes a mock impressed face, then several other taunting gestures. Johnny tries to resist, but cannot. He begins to laugh. They briefly roughhouse. As their antics subside, Johnny reaches over and touches Ron's face. Embarrassed, Ron moves away.)*

RON. I'm hungry. You got anything to eat in this place? I

mean, you make a million bucks a year and there's nothing to eat.

JOHNNY. What are you talking about? I've got a refrigerator full of stuff.

RON. Well, Jesus, Johnny, I don't mean to be rude, but a guy could die of starvation here. *(Johnny starts for the refrigerator.)*

JOHNNY. I'll rustle up something.

RON. Johnny.

JOHNNY. It'll just take a minute. I'm good at instant stuff ...

RON. Johnny! *(Johnny stops.)* I want you to kill me. You're the only one I got who loves me. Please, Johnny. Kill me. Take me to the cherry orchard. *(The brothers remain in silhouette as the lights crossfade to the interior of an airplane. The sudden loud Whoosh! of a takeoff. Lindsay and Nate sit side by side in first class. They both have drinks.)*

NATE. You see that stewardess? I could have her if I wanted her. I've got special skills with the fly babes. They hear I'm in show business, they get in line at the condom machine.

LINDSAY. Nate, you are such an unpromising teenager.

NATE. I flew one time from Atlanta to Tampa. Just a hop, right? There was this dusty blond. We'll call her Dusty.

LINDSAY. Quick. Let me write that down. *(Nate laughs. He enjoys taunting this woman.)*

NATE. Anyway, we got chatting. I was like the only guy in first class who was worth talking to.

LINDSAY. Really? What was it? One of those refugee flights?

NATE. So this leads to that. And that leads to this. And before you know it, the two of us are in this hotel suite in Tampa. We screw. It isn't exactly Gable and Lombard, but we both moan at the right time ...

LINDSAY. God, you can be revolting ...

NATE. So we're lying around afterwards and Dusty says to me, "I've never done this before." I don't believe her, but it kind of flatters me. She gets up, walks across the room. Naked. Gorgeous body. Legs that start around her neck somewhere.

LINDSAY. Dusty must have had trouble keeping her balance.

NATE. Hey, you want to hear this story or what?

LINDSAY. No!

NATE. She goes in the bathroom. So I'm thinking, "She's in there freshening herself up for a second go-round. You know, doing whatever it is that women do in hotel bathrooms mid-coitum ..."

LINDSAY. Why don't you just shut up.

NATE. No, get this. You'll like it. You'll enjoy it. Five minutes later, she comes out. You'll never guess what as.

LINDSAY. "What as?"

NATE. Guess.

LINDSAY. Please.

NATE. *(A hint of triumph.) Conan the Barbarian.*

LINDSAY. What?!

NATE. *Conan the Barbarian.* Honest to God. I mean, I didn't recognize it at first. I thought the broad had flipped. She goes into the bathroom naked, she comes out dressed as a quasi-crypto-Viking warrior. Then she starts talking in this Arnold Schwarzenegger accent. *(Imitating Schwarzenegger.)* "I'm a barbarian. You have ravaged my people. I'll be back." *(Totally serious.)* I was astounded. You've heard the word, "agape"? I was goddamn agape. "What the hell are you doing?" I said. "I'm Conan the Barbarian," she said. "What do you think, Nate? Do you think I have talent?" And then it hits me. The broad is auditioning! Dusty is auditioning! She knows I'm a producer. She figures I'm her ticket to stardom. Most incredible thing I ever saw.

LINDSAY. Do you expect me to believe that crap? *(Nate has her where he wants her.)*

NATE. Sure. Why not? Wasn't it you and all the other geniuses over at Golden Mirror who believed that I didn't know Stephen Dedalus was a pseudonym?

LINDSAY. *(Taken off-guard.)* Huh?

NATE. You think I would have committed two hundred and fifty grand of my own money if I didn't know Johnny Simmons was the guy who wrote *Mrs. Sedgewick's Head?* C'mon, Ms. McCall, smell the dailies.

LINDSAY. You knew?

NATE. Of course I knew. Big deal Arthur Winter! You tell

Artie next time you two modem each other, or whatever the hell you studio execs do in place of communication, that sending some lightweight kid like Lincoln Andrich to try and negotiate with Nathaniel Beck is an insult. *(A contemptuous laugh.)* Lincoln Andrich.... Please! I was getting fucked in this town when Lincoln Andrich still thought Snap, Crackle, and Pop lived in his cereal bowl. *(A final shot.)* Don't send a boy to do a man's job. *(Again, there is the Whoosh! of a plane landing as the lights quickly crossfade to Cahill.)*

CAHILL. *(To the audience.)* I had a client once, we'll call him Harry. He was a playwright who specialized in frothy domestic comedies. You know the sort: some trivial marital misunderstanding results in two hours of Philistine giggling. Puns. Double entendres. That sort of ... grisliness. *(Reflectively.)* One of Harry's plays, a minor Broadway triumph, I sold to the movies. Harry was retained as screenwriter. In his forties, menopausal, and callously desperate for change, he impetuously divorced his wife, disowned three children, moved to Hollywood, rented a split-level ranch in Studio City, and proceeded to turn his entire life upside-down. After submitting his first draft, he was "replaced" by the Studio. A fairly standard procedure, but Harry called me, devastated, feeling profoundly betrayed. I said, "What do you expect me to do, Harry? They want someone else." He cried on the phone, fired me, and disappeared from my life. *(Sadly.)* Four years later, he resurfaced. He was selling souvlaki, lamb on a spit, at a grubby stand off Sixth Avenue. When I saw him, I could feel the blood go out of my face. He didn't seem to recognize me. Indeed, as I stood staring, he said, "Hey, you! You in the suit! Get your ass out of the fancy joints and take a chance on some good honest street food. Take a chance on life!" Then he laughed, maniacally in my opinion. *(A final pause.)* Two blocks away, I thought of some clever rejoinder. But I never went back. When Hollywood gets in their veins and metastasizes, I never go back. *(The lights fade on Cahill and come up quickly on Johnny's bedroom: a stark space with a bed, a desk, a typewriter. Not dissimilar to a prison cell. Johnny sits on the bed, still wearing plain gray clothes. Cara is in the doorway.)*

CARA. They're here, Johnny.

JOHNNY. Who did they send?

CARA. That producer, Nathaniel Beck, and a woman from the studio. I told them you'd be down.

JOHNNY. What are they like?

CARA. I don't know.... Well dressed. Pleasant. I don't know.

JOHNNY. The woman, is she flashy, toothy, and soul-less? Or drab, tight-lipped, and soul-less?

CARA. I don't know, Johnny.

JOHNNY. *(Suddenly alarmed.)* You didn't tell them about my leg?

CARA. No. I didn't tell them much of anything. They just got here.

JOHNNY. I'm tired of people talking about it. It happened in prison. Things happen in there. Terrible things.

CARA. What should I tell them? Are you coming down?

JOHNNY. They can wait awhile. We can talk, can't we?

CARA. Sure, honey. We can talk. *(Gently, Cara approaches and sits next to him on the bed. Johnny lapses into a long dead silence. Cara finally breaks it.)* Those people are waiting for you. They've come a long way.

JOHNNY. I'm not doing the screenplay. I told Cahill that.

CARA. I know. But you have to tell them yourself. They don't want me or Cahill to tell them. They need it to be you.

JOHNNY. Of course. A meeting. They covet a meeting. They worship at the altar of the meeting. *(A decision.)* Tell them I'll see them tomorrow.

CARA. They plan on leaving tonight.

JOHNNY. We'll put them up in the guest room.

CARA. Johnny, they won't stay.

JOHNNY. They'll stay, *Cara mia.* They smell the money. If they smell the money, they always stay. *(The lights quickly crossfade to the kitchen. Nate and Lindsay, obviously waiting, look around them. Nate is pacing, manic. They both have coffee. Their overnight luggage is placed near the front door.)*

NATE. Well, here we are, Ms. McCall. Amityville North. Did you see the way that Cara broad looked at us?

LINDSAY. Give it a rest, Nate. You practically drove the cab driver mad.

NATE. I drove him mad? I drove him mad?! Why? Because I had the balls to ask him if he'd mind removing the road-kill he had stored in his trunk? The deceased mammals he intended on putting our luggage on top of?

LINDSAY. Big deal. He had a few dead animals in the trunk. He explained the whole thing.

NATE. Yeah. Right. He found them on his route, took them home, skinned them, and sold them wholesale to a local furrier. Highly credible.

LINDSAY. That wasn't the story.

NATE. Close enough.

LINDSAY. We'll be on the plane again in a couple of hours. Then you can continue to torture the airline personnel.

NATE. Torture? They serve bay scallops at thirty-thousand feet over Nebraska and call them "fresh from the sea"? Who's torturing who?

LINDSAY. Nate, do us both a favor.

NATE. Shut up, right?

LINDSAY. I was thinking more like "drop dead."

NATE. *(Needs one last shot.)* And whether you noticed it or not, that cab driver you're so fond of had a growth on his forehead that made me think of Charles Laughton in *The Hunchback of Notre Dame.* Tell me we're not in some Gothic Hell here! One of those places where so many cousins are screwing so many other cousins that after three generations everybody ends up with one huge eye and feet shaped like pine cones. *(Lindsay cannot help herself. She bursts into laughter. Nate joins in, aware of his own absurdity. Eddie enters from outside. He holds a large elaborately carved birdhouse. A long moment as the three just look to each other.)*

EDDIE. If there's anything sadder than a yard without a birdhouse, I don't know what it is. Jeepers! *(A moment.)* Hi. You people are from the film studio, right? I'm Eddie. Eddie Stopanokovitch. People call me Eddie Stop.

LINDSAY. Hi. I'm Lindsay McCall. This is Nate Beck.

EDDIE. *(Shaking hands.)* Eddie Stopanokovitch. People call me Eddie Stop.

NATE. *(Shaking.)* Nate Beck.

EDDIE. Eddie Stopanokovitch. People call me Eddie Stop.

NATE. Nate Beck. People call me Nate Beck.

EDDIE. Oh.... Oh, I get it. Jeepers! Yeah. Yeah. Jeepers! No, I do that. I repeat. Jeepers!

NATE. *(Looking heavenward.)* Beam me up, Scottie.

EDDIE. Where's Cara?

LINDSAY. Upstairs? She went to tell Mr. Simmons that we were here.

EDDIE. Johnny won't meet you people, you know.

NATE. Why's that?.

EDDIE. *(A shrug.)* I'm the caretaker. I mean, there ain't all that much to fix, but Johnny likes a caretaker.

LINDSAY. Why won't he meet us?

EDDIE. Weirdness probably. His hook's run out of bait. *(The three benignly study each other. Finally, made nervous by silence, Eddie holds up the birdhouse.)* He likes birdhouses. I've got a martins' house out back that you wouldn't believe. It's like a palace. A bird palace. *(Needs to chatter.)* I love working with wood. It started when I was a kid. Dad was a picker. We'd hang out at the dump, scarf some neat stuff, come home, build stuff. I've got a childhood rich with how-to memories. Jeepers! In my parents' yard, there were maybe twenty birdhouses. So one time, the mailman asks my Dad, "How come you got so many birdhouses?" *(Laughs.)* People, huh? *(Indicating the coffee.)* You folks like me to warm up your cup?

LINDSAY. Thanks.

EDDIE. What about you there, Nate Beck?

NATE. Sure. Why not? *(Eddie pours them each coffee.)*

EDDIE. I once made seventeen shadow boxes in a nine hour stretch.

LINDSAY. *(Politely.)* Really? I think I made one once in high school. I don't know whatever happened to it.

EDDIE. You know what they used to call my house? "Knickknackville." Honest. "Knickknackville." My Dad, he saved everything. *(Thinks about this.)* For as long as I can remember, we had bales of wire in the bathroom. Hub caps on the kitchen walls. Chairs. We once had maybe forty chairs in the living room. Dad piled them one on top of the other. It looked funny, but we never wanted for a place to sit. *(Lindsay and Nate steal a glance.)* We had one-hundred and sixty-three sets of salt and pepper shakers. The kids thought that was funny. So I'd ask them, "How many salt and pepper shakers do you guys have?" "One," they'd say. "Two," they'd say. Jeepers! People, huh?

NATE. Look, Eddie, you wouldn't have any idea when Cara might be down?

EDDIE. Nope. You know, while you're waiting, maybe you'd like to see the martins' house. I'll get it. It ain't on its pole yet.

LINDSAY. That'd be nice. Thanks.

EDDIE. The martin, he's a peculiar bird. If he can't see three-hundred and sixty degrees, he won't nest. A real paranoid one. I'll be right back. Relax. Take a load off your shoulders. *(Eddie cheerfully exits.)*

NATE. Okay? What is it? Do they call him, "Eddie Stop?" Or do they tell him, "Eddie, stop!"

LINDSAY. He was just trying to be nice.

NATE. Somebody should tell him *Green Acres* is off the air.

LINDSAY. What is it, Nate? If somebody doesn't wear an Armani and a Rolex, they're not good enough for you?

NATE. So who are you? The Revolutionary Voice of the People? Don't give me that bullshit. Your idea of mingling with the proletariat is renting a Benz instead of hiring a limo.

LINDSAY. You're right. I apologize for behaving like a human being.

NATE. No problem. It happens. *(Cara appears on the landing. She descends the stairway.)* Well?

CARA. He won't see you.

NATE. What?

CARA. Johnny's not ... feeling well. It'll have to wait until the morning.

NATE. This is a joke, right?

LINDSAY. Nate.

NATE. No, please. I have to know. This is what they call "rural humor", am I right on this?

CARA. It's not a joke, Mr. Beck. He can't see you until the morning.

LINDSAY. We have reservations to return to New York tonight.

CARA. I know. I'm sorry. I truly am. You can stay here for the night. He'll be ... fine ... better ... in the morning.

NATE. Here? What? Are we wearing buckskins? Do we look like the kind of people accustomed to circling the wagons, eating the buffalo, and fending off the ...

LINDSAY. Nate, please!

CARA. The closest motel is almost fifty miles away.

LINDSAY. And you're sure he can't be persuaded?

CARA. Johnny's not persuadable.

NATE. *(Positively frenetic.)* Fine. Terrific. Perfect. This'll go in the autobiography. I guarantee you. This will appear in my autobiography ...

LINDSAY. Nate, will you give it a rest!

NATE. Chapter nineteen: "Meeting the Great Man in Bohunkville!" *(Before anybody can respond to this pronouncement, Eddie enters from outside. Talking. He proudly carries a huge fastidiously carved and painted martins' house. It's a superb piece of craftsmanship.)*

EDDIE. Jeepers! Martins! Jeepers! A martin won't nest anywhere where he hasn't got a clear view of his total environment. Some people call the martin, "Nature's Flying Paranoic."

NATE. Where's the remote?! Give me the fucking remote!

LINDSAY. Shut up, Nate! Jesus! Just shut up!! *(Silence. Neither Cara nor Eddie know what to make of these two. Embarrassed, Lindsay turns to them.)* I'm sorry. I just.... We're just.... It's been a long trip and this is quite a disappointment. I apologize. I particularly apologize for ... my colleague's behavior.

NATE. She's right. I'm sorry. It's not your fault. I apologize.

EDDIE. Water under the hassock.

NATE. Huh?

EDDIE. Just a common phrase.

NATE. *(Irrationally.)* "Water under the hassock," is not a common phrase. "Water under the bridge," is a common phrase. "A stitch in time saves nine," is a common phrase. "What goes around comes around," is a common phrase. "Water under the hassock," is only a common phrase in places where people live with water in their goddamn living rooms! It is not, not, a common phrase!

LINDSAY. Jesus, Nate.

EDDIE. Oh yeah? Jeepers! Well, what about, "A penny saved is a penny earned?"

NATE. What about it?

EDDIE. *(Dumbly.)* I don't know …

NATE. *(To Lindsay.)* Do you follow this? Am I dreaming?

LINDSAY. Forget it, please.

EDDIE. And it's not, "What goes around comes around." It's, "What goes around will come back to haunt you." *(Unnoticed, Johnny appears on the landing. He watches silently.)*

NATE. "What goes around comes around." That's the phrase.

EDDIE. "What goes around will come back to haunt you."

NATE. "What goes around comes around!"

LINDSAY. Let it go, Nate. This is …

NATE. "Water under the hassock!" Don't make me laugh.

EDDIE. "What goes around comes around!" Don't make me laugh.

NATE. "Shove it up your ass!" How's that? Common enough?!

LINDSAY. *(Together with Cara.)* Nate, shut up!

CARA. *(Together with Lindsay.)* Stop it, Eddie!

JOHNNY. *(From above, cutting through.)* "In Dallas, the buildings pop out of the flatness like iridescent toast." *(Silence. They all watch as Johnny comes downstairs. He visibly struggles with a limp. He approaches Lindsay and Nate. He shakes both of their hands. They are intimidated.)* I'm Johnny Simmons.

LINDSAY. Lindsay McCall. Hi.

NATE. Nate Beck. My pleasure.

JOHNNY. I had that common phrase taped over my desk for years. Just waiting for the right time, the right place. This was it. *(A charming smile.)* I won't be able to discuss the project tonight. We'll try in the morning. You can stay here. *(A look to Eddie.)* We'll keep Eddie chained and gagged. *(Johnny turns and starts up the stairs, leaving as quietly as he had arrived.)*

NATE. Look, we kind of had other plans. This won't take long.

CARA. Johnny can't do it tonight.
NATE. Let him tell me. He's right here.
LINDSAY. He's already told you!
EDDIE. Water under the hassock.
NATE. Jesus!
JOHNNY. Water under the bridge.
NATE. Exactly! That's what I've been trying to tell him.
JOHNNY. "Water under the hassock," should be water under the bridge. Wouldn't you agree with that, Mr. Beck?
CARA. *(Seeing something coming.)* Johnny ...
JOHNNY. Let bygones be bygones. Let sleeping dogs lie.
NATE. Look, how about we try to do business here?
CARA. I keep telling you, Mr. Beck ...
NATE. Frankly, we're not prepared to stay over. We haven't had our shots updated.
LINDSAY. Jesus, Nate ...
JOHNNY. *(Cold as ice.)* Tell me, Mr. Beck, do you think you're the first Hollywood hustler I've ever met?
NATE. Look, I'm sorry. I apologize. I just didn't phrase things properly. I know you're a man of considerable experience. I appreciate that. And I sympathize if you're not feeling ...
JOHNNY. We'll discuss the deal tomorrow. If that doesn't fit in with your plans, then so be it. Ten A.M. *(Johnny continues up. Nate looks around him impotently, crazed.)*
NATE. Christ, for all we know, you didn't even write the goddamn thing! Memorized it in prison.... Bullshit! You're so goddamned fragile you can barely remember yesterday! *(Johnny is stopped in his tracks. He turns. The others are frozen as he comes back onto the landing. He begins to speak, quoting from* Mrs. Sedgewick's Head.*)*
JOHNNY. I can remember yesterday, Mr. Beck. I can remember every goddamn word! *(Begins to quote.)*

"When I was twelve, my best friend was a kid named Bobby Sedgewick. He was bony and tall and had an air of incipient loneliness. One cloudless night, his parents gathered us in their black Hudson Hornet and took us to a traveling carnival. The mother had a kind of elongated head. And the father had a left arm that worked only at right angles. They were … misshapen people. *(Johnny comes down into the main room. As he does so, the lights gradually fade. Carnival music begins softly in the background. The others become mere onlookers. It is the past.)*

"After awhile, we went into one of the freak tents. 'Nature Betrayed!' it promised. There was a fat lady and a fat man and a woman with a beard and a midget who swallowed swords taller than himself. And then there were all these things in bottles. A snake with two heads. A calf with five feet. Tortoises without shells. But then, there were these babies. Premature babies with too many arms and no eyes and backs stuck together. All in formaldehyde. And Bobby's parents were saying, 'Look at this one,' and, 'See their little hands,' and other generally moronic observations…. And I started to cry. *(Stars appear: bright and twinkling and filling the stage.)*

"So Bobby's parents took me outside and they tried to be nice. And I remember looking up at Mrs. Sedgewick, and the lights were such that her elongated head was lit against a dark sky, and thinking, 'This lady has the weirdest head I've ever seen,' and then it happened. Right behind that deformed head, millions of miles away, trapped in the primordial past, was a meteor shower: this grand explosion of light flashing across the sky. *(A shower of light streaks across the blackness. Johnny looks up.)*

"And, as I looked up, right in the middle of it was the longest head in captivity. And this head, Mrs. Sedgewick's head, said to me, 'Don't cry about those babies. They travel all over the country. Believe me, they'll see a lot more of the world than you or me or Mr. Sedgewick or maybe even President Eisenhower himself.' And that, that small incident, that sliver of images caught in a meteor shower, is when I learned about irony. *(Carnival lights appear, those weak pastels found in traveling shows. A huge 50's canvas mural drops down. On it are the words, "Nature Betrayed!" It has artfully drawn caricatures of sideshow freaks and oddities. An explosion of light, as if a star had been smashed by a hammer. For a long moment, the stage is eerily bright. The vast canvas poster seems luminescent. Johnny stands motionlessly, looking up, mouth agape.)*

"Irony is babies in jars, stars cascading across the sky, moist carnival earth underneath, and Mrs. Sedgewick's head." *(Nate, Cara, Eddie, and Lindsay have all disappeared from the stage. It is Johnny alone in the midst of this pyrotechnic past.)*

BLACKOUT

END OF ACT ONE

ACT TWO

Silent film theme music plays as images of Charlie Chaplin* and Albert Einstein* fill the screen. Wearing a cast on one arm, Cahill watches. When the montage is done, he turns outward.*

CAHILL. *(To the audience.)* There is a tale, perhaps apocryphal, that Charlie Chaplin invited Albert Einstein to be his guest at the premiere of *City Lights.* Just think! Chaplin! Einstein! It was in those feverish younger days when gala openings were events that lifted the communal spirit. After the film, they emerged from the theatre. Adoring fans screamed their adulation. They crushed forward. They threw themselves against the velvet ropes. They tossed flowers and mementos. Chaplin smiled, waved, then disappeared into the studio limousine. Mr. Einstein, ingenuously unaccustomed to these naked displays of public affection, turned to Mr. Chaplin. "What does this all mean?" he asked. Chaplin looked at him sadly. "Nothing," he said. *(The lights fade on Cahill and bump up quickly on Arthur's office. A very defensive Lincoln stands across from the seated Arthur. Simmering, Arthur leafs through a stack of papers.)*
ARTHUR. So, Lincoln, explain yourself.
LINCOLN. It was a stupid thing to do. *(Nothing.)* I just lost ... control. I thought I was doing the right thing and obviously, I'd ... I'm very sorry, Arthur.
ARTHUR. Let me see how I am on sequence. You found out Cahill was in town, you tracked him down, you went to his hotel, and you ingratiated yourself into his suite.
LINCOLN. I didn't ingratiate myself. I just called him and asked if I could come up for a few minutes.
ARTHUR. Then, you tried to convince this distinguished reputable man that if he jerked Nate Beck around for six months, the option on *Mrs. Sedgewick's Head* would run out.

* See Special Note on Songs and Recordings on copyright page.

At which point, we would purchase the option for an even higher amount. This would get Nate out of the way and secure a greater likelihood of the picture being made. And, finally, it would also make Lincoln Andrich a hero.

LINCOLN. I wasn't trying to be a hero. I was trying to be a businessman.

ARTHUR. But that's the gist?

LINCOLN. Hey, it's Nathaniel Beck we're talking about. The man is a total scumbag. He's been dead in this town for six years.

ARTHUR. Nate Beck is an experienced producer with sixteen films to his credit. He might not be the best or the most tasteful, but he's fought the wars, Lincoln. He's got the scars and the bruises and he's not nearly as crude or as dumb as he pretends to be.

LINCOLN. He's a hypocritical piece of showbiz deadwood. Can we please get back to work, Arthur.

ARTHUR. *(Lets this pass.)* That's the gist?

LINCOLN. Yes.

ARTHUR. And when Mr. Cahill reacted with scorn to this highly unethical maneuvering, you called him a "washed-up New York literary asshole."

LINCOLN. I told you. I just lost it. He was just so ... I don't know ... superior or something ...

ARTHUR. And then, and I find this remarkable, you hit him?

LINCOLN. I didn't hit him.

ARTHUR. He says you did.

LINCOLN. He was trying to usher me out. I just pulled my arm away. He lost his balance and he fell.

ARTHUR. He broke his arm, Lincoln!

LINCOLN. I didn't hit him! It was just an accident!

ARTHUR. He's wearing a fucking cast!

LINCOLN. *(A wise-ass smile.)* Thin old bones, I guess.

ARTHUR. Jesus ... *(A smoldering pause.)* You know, there's a common perception that the film business is ruthless and somehow, despite its glamour, sleazy.

LINCOLN. Look, Arthur, I was out of line. But I don't need

a lecture on the film business.

ARTHUR. No? How about a sentence or two? When the players in this town find out that the other players in this town are egregiously breaking the rules.... Forget beating up old men! Just egregiously breaking the rules, they don't react with shock. They just pick up their talent and go elsewhere. Is this because they're moralists? Hardly.

LINCOLN. I said I didn't need a lecture ...

ARTHUR. *(Angrily cutting through.)* It's because they don't want the same thing happening to them!

LINCOLN. So what's the big deal? I tried to make a move that'd put us in a better position. It backfired, but I'm not ashamed of it.

ARTHUR. Robert Cahill represents major writers. He isn't some itinerant hustler booking Vegas lounge acts!

LINCOLN. He's a smug old asshole. And I'm sorry I blew it, but so what about his arm? He did it himself. He never should have laid a finger on me. The superior washed-up bastard! *(Silence. The time has come.)*

ARTHUR. I almost admire you, Lincoln. Almost ... *(Bloodless.)* I'm authorizing three months severance. I'll provide a letter of recommendation. Should Mr. Cahill decide to litigate, we will do everything in our power to divorce ourselves from your behavior. You're fired. As of now. Clean out your desk and turn in your pass. Good luck. Meeting over.

LINCOLN. *(Stunned.)* What the.... You can't ...

ARTHUR. Meeting over.

LINCOLN. Who the fuck do you think ...

ARTHUR. Meeting over, Lincoln! *(As if physically assaulted, Lincoln starts to say something, but instead, almost reels to the door. He turns.)*

LINCOLN. You bastard. You goddamn phony no talent old bastard. Old! That's what you are. Old!! You're all so fucking old ... *(Lincoln exits, carefully shutting the door behind him. For a long time, Arthur sits motionless, drained.)*

ARTHUR. *(Dully, to himself.)* Yeah ... *(Arthur begins to review the papers before him as the lights crossfade to Eddie and Nate, now in shirt-sleeves. They sit outside on the front steps. The distinct sound of crickets.)*

NATE. I hate crickets. You know what crickets make me think of? Nature. Fishing, camping, shit like that. You know what fishing, camping, shit like that, makes me think of? Fishermen. I hate fishermen. They make me think of hobby shops. Don't ask me why. I hate hobby shops. Trains and stamps and wood-burning kits. They give me the creeps.

EDDIE. *(Blithely.)* God's little chickens.

NATE. What?

EDDIE. God's little chickens. Crickets. That's what my Mom called them. God's little chickens. *(Ruminates.)* My Mom had a cricket that wanted to be her pet.

NATE. Is that a fact?

EDDIE. He lived in the tub. Lived there for three days. Chirp chirp chirp. Cricket in the tub. Nicest sound you ever heard.

NATE. Until bath time.

EDDIE. Ain't it the truth. My Dad wanted his Thursday bath. My Mom said, "What about the cricket?" "I'll take him outside," Dad said. "I won't hurt him." So that's what he did. He put him right outside, took his bath, and that was that. *(Eddie stops, seemingly finished. Nate waits, then cannot stand it.)*

NATE. That's it? That's the story? Act One: Cricket in the tub. Act Two: Mom and Cricket fall in love. Act Three: Cricket takes a hike. That's it?

EDDIE. The next night, My Mom gets up to go to the bathroom. Poor Mom had a bladder like a vegetable strainer. And lo and behold, there's the cricket. Back in the tub. Jeepers! She wakes up my father. "The cricket's back," she said. "I'll throw him out in the morning," Dad says. *(Another pause. Nate conspicuously checks his watch.)*

NATE. So how did the cricket get back in the house? Mom give him an extra key?

EDDIE. Nope. We'll never know. Just one of those things.

NATE. Uh huh. Maybe PBS can do a special.

EDDIE. Next morning, Dad takes the cricket and puts him outside on the flagstone path. Mom's at the window. And she and Dad ... they were kinda fooling around ... waved goodbye to the cricket as he hopped his way down the path. *(A storyteller's zeal.)* Just then, swooping down out of the sky, comes this mockingbird. Screechscreechscreech! And there's the cricket. Hophophop. And there's the bird. Swoopswoopswoop. Then! Zoom! The mockingbird eats the cricket! Chompchompchomp! Unbelievable! Jeepers! I'll never forget it. God's little chickens. *(Eddie is finished. Nate studies him with a measure of mystification.)*

NATE. So what's the point?

EDDIE. The point? Jeepers! It's as plain as the ears on your head.

NATE. The nose on my face.

EDDIE. Ears on your head.

NATE. Nose on my face!

EDDIE. Half a dozen of one. Half a dozen of the other.

NATE. Jeepers!! *(The lights quickly crossfade from Nate and Eddie to Arthur and Cahill, both on the phone. Wearing headphones, Arthur is at one side of the stage. Cahill, still wearing a cast, is at the other.)*

ARTHUR. We've dismissed Mr. Andrich. I hope you don't confuse his ... aggressiveness ... with the posture of The Studio. This has been an embarrassment.

CAHILL. Please, Arthur. I didn't interrupt your schedule to discuss Mr. Andrich.

ARTHUR. You didn't?

CAHILL. *(This is difficult terrain.)* I received a call from Johnny Simmons. I understand your people are visiting him?

ARTHUR. Right. They should be back in New York by now.

CAHILL. Apparently, they're not. Have you spoken with them?

ARTHUR. No. Not yet.

CAHILL. I didn't know whether to ... Mr. Simmons is a client and I'm reluctant to suggest ...

ARTHUR. What?

CAHILL. Johnny sounded, I don't know, peculiar. Which, if you know him, is not unusual, but ...

ARTHUR. What'd he say, Robert?

CAHILL. He said, and maybe he was just joking ... I mean, the man does have a rather baroque sense of humor. Positively

Byzantine. He said, "Tell Arthur I'll do the screenplay if he gives me the girl. A straight-up unconditional trade."

ARTHUR. An unconditional trade...?

CAHILL. As I said, Byzantine.

ARTHUR. What'd he mean?

CAHILL. What could he mean?

ARTHUR. With him? Christ, almost anything.

CAHILL. I'm afraid that's what he meant.

ARTHUR. What?

CAHILL. Almost anything. *(The lights crossfade on the men and come up quickly on a small, ugly, knotty pine bedroom dominated by an ancient maple children's bunkbed. Nate sits on the top bunk, his stuff strewn beside him. Lindsay, in a long nightshirt and looking exhausted, lies on the bottom bunk. They are two very unhappy campers.)*

NATE. And, by the way, while you were chit-chatting with Sir Arthur Winter, His Hollywood Holiness, I was outside with my new best chum, Eddie. You know, sharing all those things we have in common. Male bonding in Okie Hell. *(Lindsay seems on the verge of screaming. Nate looks around with wonder.)* In New York, I stay at The Pierre. In LA, I recommend The Wilshire, The Four Seasons ... maybe The Marquis. And when I'm in upstate New York, I stay here. Voilà!

LINDSAY. Nate, Jesus ...

NATE. Knotty pine purgatory!

LINDSAY. Please ...

NATE. Bunkbeds! A stench of mold so strong my lungs are turning into mushrooms!

LINDSAY. God! You refused to stay at the only motel within fifty miles.

NATE. Yeah, right. I'm going to stay in a motel where Anthony Perkins is the desk clerk.

LINDSAY. A woman answered the phone.

NATE. Bullshit. It was Anthony Perkins pretending to be his mother.

LINDSAY. Please, Nate. Let me just sleep.

NATE. Fine. Sleep. *(Nate jumps down from the upper bunk. He begins to pace.)* I told you he was a lunatic. I told you. "It'll be an adventure," you said. Some adventure. He can't talk business until the sun is in the morning sky. We would've done better negotiating with the Peruvian fucking Incas.

LINDSAY. He's obviously a mess, but we're here to try to convince him. If that takes some ... patience, well ...

NATE. Patience! Please. Patience is waiting in line at the bank. This guy requires thorazine.

LINDSAY. And I think antagonizing him was just plain stupid.

NATE. Me antagonize him?! *(A moment.)* You're right. It was. It was real moron time. It's like just being here is disintegrating my neurons every goddamn rustic second.

LINDSAY. *(After a pause.)* What did you think of Cara?

NATE. "It's not nice to fool Mother Nature."

LINDSAY. Do you think maybe they have ... I don't know, a relationship?

NATE. A relationship? You mean do I think they screw? Let me tell you something, Ms. McCall, the only sex going on around here is when the mice and the skunks and the raccoons and the other nocturnal beasts that thrive in this Davy Crockett environment get on top of each other by accident on their way to the decompression chamber.

LINDSAY. Would you mind repeating that, Nate? You know, for those of us who cherish English?

NATE. Okay. I admit it. It didn't make any sense. *(Nate sits next to her. And for the first time, he seems legitimately worn. Reflective.)* I got a twelve-year-old kid. I haven't seem him in six months. His mother and he live in Arkansas. Can you believe that? Arkansas. It's like a sadistic prank. I mean, I write and I call and send presents and.... But it isn't the same, you know? I mean, you get a divorce to get away from the harridan you married, and instead you end up getting a divorce from your kid. *(Getting up again.)* I pay so much alimony, she probably owns Arkansas by now. Of course, what's to own? The alfalfa co-op? The porcupine farm? I mean, who the fuck knows? Arkansas. *(Thinks about this.)* You ever been married?

LINDSAY. Once.

NATE. And?

LINDSAY. And nothing. And now I'm not.

NATE. You involved? Gay? Neutered? Diseased? Anything? *(Nothing.)* Hey, it's the nineties. I ask.

LINDSAY. *(Resembling admiration.)* Nate Beck, you are a piece of work.

NATE. I mean, here we are. You. Me. A zillion miles from civilization. You're not married. I'm not married ...

LINDSAY. You don't mean...?

NATE. Sure. Sex. What else is there to do here? Whittle?

LINDSAY. Nate, if you were the last living thing on earth ...

NATE. Don't give me that high and mighty bullshit. If Arthur Winter were here, you'd be wearing baby doll pajamas and cooing ... *(Just occurs to him.)* So what is it with you and Arthur anyway?

LINDSAY. *(A resentful edge.)* Nothing. I work for the man.

NATE. You mean to tell me he's never hit on you? C'mon.

LINDSAY. I told you. We have a professional relationship.

NATE. Bullshit. Arthur Winter is an oversexed sleazeball just like the rest of us. He sees a piece of ass, the man needs to be physically restrained. You should see him at Cannes. You ever go to Cannes?

LINDSAY. Nate, you're not giving me a migraine. You are a migraine.

NATE. Cannes! What a farce! "The world community of film ..." Bullshit! You know what Cannes' about?

LINDSAY. Let me guess.

NATE. Middle aged men ogling young international breasts.

LINDSAY. Middle aged men ogling young international breasts.

NATE. Bingo! *(Lindsay has had it. She throws a blazer on over her nightshirt and starts to leave.)* Where you going?

LINDSAY. I can't take it any more.

NATE. Fine. You don't want to chat, we won't chat.

LINDSAY. You don't chat, Nate. You babble. You spit out streams of invective that make no sense. You bitch because people don't return your calls. Big surprise! Who wants to listen to this irredeemable crap?

NATE. What's the matter? Afraid I'll tell you some Arthur Winter stories that'll curdle your blood?

LINDSAY. Jesus, please, just shut up.
NATE. Remember that bimbo he tried to hype about three years ago? Used to be Miss Norway? Helga Dipshit or whatever her name was? Ask your boss someday whether or not Helga talks in her sleep.
LINDSAY. *(Level and hard.)* Fuck you, Nate. *(Lindsay exits. Nate stares at the closed door, then comes forward.)*
NATE. *(To the audience.)* Helga ... what? I don't remember. She had so much silicone in her body, she was afraid of radiators. *(A long moment.)* She's right. I used to be a person. Really. It's hard to believe. When I first came to LA, I had aspirations. Hopes. Dreams. I actually used "quality" in a sentence once. *(Long pause. Nate turns away from the audience and surveys this grisly little room. As if an afterthought, he turns back.)* Two years ago, the last day of the season, my kid, Tommy, pitches two innings and he strikes out six kids in a row. Bang bang bang. Like this munchkin Roger Clemens or somebody. Afterwards, we were leaving the field, and we were laughing and joking and.... And he looked at me, and he smiled that miracle of a smile, and he said, "Dad, this is the life." And it was. *(Raw honesty.)* And now he lives in a place called Arkansas with a woman I once adored and I see him twice a year if I'm lucky ... Hollywood. *(The lights crossfade to Johnny's kitchen. Wearing a ratty old bathrobe, Cara sits at the table, reading a magazine and nursing a drink. Not her first. Lindsay comes down the stairs. She and Cara share a look.)*
CARA. Couldn't sleep?
LINDSAY. Being alone in a bedroom with Nate Beck is not conducive to sleep. Or any other traditional form of human behavior.
CARA. You want a drink? I'm one of those secret late night drinkers.
LINDSAY. No thanks. I could use some coffee though.
CARA. Help yourself. Doesn't it keep you awake?
LINDSAY. I'm already awake. *(Lindsay starts to prepare instant coffee. Cara watches intently. Lindsay becomes aware of her.)* What?
CARA. You're just one of those people who looks great no matter what they're wearing, doing, whatever. It's horrifying.

LINDSAY. You wouldn't think that if you'd just been hit on by a maniacal film producer.

CARA. Maybe you're right.

LINDSAY. Not maybe. I am right.

CARA. I don't know. The last time I was officially "hit on", it was by a man whose claim to fame was that he'd lost his spleen in a hunting accident.

LINDSAY. Really?

CARA. Really. His name was, get this, Cecil Meecel.

LINDSAY. *(Laughing.)* You're making that up.

CARA. Nope. Cecil Meecel. He worked at the local tile factory. He smelled like a motel bathroom. A loathsome man with a loathsome smell and no spleen.

LINDSAY. How did you brush him off?

CARA. I divorced the bastard. *(Both women laugh. Lindsay sits.)*

LINDSAY. Actually, Nate isn't all bad. He just won't shut up. *(Carefully.)* So what's a nice girl like you doing in a place like this?

CARA. Protecting Johnny from the wolves.

LINDSAY. From what I've heard, Johnny doesn't need all that much protecting.

CARA. You've heard wrong.

LINDSAY. How did you get the job?

CARA. When he got out of prison, he needed a secretary/mother/maid/confessor. The hours are long. The responsibilities are horrendous.

LINDSAY. But you stay.

CARA. But I stay.

LINDSAY. Why?

CARA. Because I love him.

LINDSAY. Oh.... Didn't Cecil object to that?

CARA. Cecil didn't much care about what I did. As long as supper was on the table and he could find his spleen supplements or whatever the hell they were.

LINDSAY. And what did Johnny think of Cecil?

CARA. He referred to him as, "Larry Linoleum, Alleged Mammal." *(A silly grin.)* Right to his face sometimes. Cecil didn't have a clue.

LINDSAY. And what did Cecil think of Johnny?
CARA. *(A statement of fact.)* He thought he was a murderer. *(The lights rapidly fade, then bump up on Johnny. It is the past. He sits alone on the porch, turning the pistol over and over in his hands. Ron enters from inside the house. Weak, he has wrapped himself in a* Winnie the Pooh *comforter. He carries a battered paperback novel.)*
RON. Hi.
JOHNNY. Hi.
RON. Winnie the Pooh. I never liked him. Him or that kid that always hung around him. What was that kid's name?
JOHNNY. Christopher Robin?
RON. Yeah. Christopher Robin. I never liked him. An awful dweeb of a kid, don't you think?
JOHNNY. I can't go through with this, Ron. I really can't.
RON. Johnny, we been talking about this for hours. *(Suddenly.)* It's cold here. It's always cold here. You'd think a guy like you, you'd live in Florida. Florida is full of snakes. I heard one time about a guy getting bit by a coral snake at a carwash. In Tallahassee or someplace. He was dead before the rinse cycle. *(Reflectively.)* Tallahassee. Imagine being a kid and you had to learn to spell Tallahassee because you lived there. "Now, boys and girls, we're going to learn to spell Tallahassee." I would have thrown up in despair ... *(Erratically.)* Hey, what is a dweeb anyway?
JOHNNY. Huh?
RON. Dweeb. I just said that ... *(Confused.)* Jesus! Winnie the Pooh's friend, what was his name?
JOHNNY. Christopher Robin?
RON. Yeah. I just said that Christopher Robin was a dweeb. But, what is a dweeb anyway? I mean, I hear people say it and stuff, but, "Dweeb." What is that?
JOHNNY. I don't know. Jesus, Ron, I can't do this!
RON. *(Irrationally.)* You're the writer! You're supposed to know stuff like that! That's your goddamn job, isn't it?
JOHNNY. No. People who make the dictionaries, that's their job.
RON. Then what's your job?
JOHNNY. I take the dictionaries and I rearrange the words

in non-alphabetical order. *(This stops Ron. He considers the observation very carefully. He hands Johnny the book.)*
RON. I want you to read that thing about how it was when we were kids. You know, over my body. I'd like that, Johnny. My eulogy kind of. I'd really like that. *(Johnny studies the book. It is as if he'd never seen it before.)*
JOHNNY. I haven't looked at this thing in years.
RON. Your first book, Johnny. Mom and Dad, they were so proud of you. I mean, the only books we ever had in the house were those, you know, supermarket encyclopedia things. And then there was this. Your book.
JOHNNY. It's a pretty lousy book.
RON. They loved that fucking book! *(The anger already gone.)* Those supermarket encyclopedias ... God, they were fun, huh? Like too bad we never got beyond the G's or the J's or something. Remember? Volume I was where it frequently stopped for us. So you'd get too much stuff about archery or anacondas ...
JOHNNY. And not a goddamn thing about ...
RON. Reproduction. Intercourse. *(Laughs.)* Vagina.
JOHNNY. You were a twisted kid.
RON. Hey, when you stop thinking about vaginas, it's time to throw in the towel. *(Starkly.)* I've stopped thinking about that stuff, Johnny. *(The lights rapidly crossfade to the kitchen. Cara finishes her drink.)*
CARA. Three hours later, they walked to the cherry orchard. Johnny shot Ron. End of story.
LINDSAY. Did Johnny tell you all this?
CARA. Who else? *(Silently, Cara clears away her stuff. She takes off the bathrobe and puts it away, preparing to leave. She throws on a coat.)* I don't mean to be anti-social. I just have to get some sleep. You people might need a ... translator in the morning.
LINDSAY. Sure.
CARA. Help yourself.
LINDSAY. Thanks. *(Cara starts for the front door.)* Cara? You never told me how you got the job.
CARA. No. I never did.
LINDSAY. *(A self-conscious laugh.)* I might as well ask. Are

you and Johnny lovers?

CARA. That would be pretty perverse, wouldn't it?

LINDSAY. I don't know. I mean ...

CARA. Johnny Simmons is my brother. *(Cara exits. Lindsay remains at the table as the lights crossfade to Lincoln. Jangling music erupts as he glides onto the stage wearing* a de rigueur *skating outfit. Replete with headphones. He is roller blading. He stops.)*

LINCOLN. *(To the audience.)* I exercise twice a day, six days a week. On Sundays, I read scripts. But only the first six pages. I can tell by then whether it's a movie or the usual literary drivel. Really. I look for adverbs. Writers who gratuitously use adverbs should be summarily shot. I go to a health club in the mornings. I roller-blade or play squash in the late afternoons. I always have trouble finding squash partners. Everybody's always busy. *(With pride.)* I don't have social friends, but I do the industry parties and screenings and kissy-face bullshit with the best of them. I've met more important people in this town in three years than most people meet in a lifetime. *(Utterly serious.)* Just wait. I'll be back. And I'll get the creep. I'll blindside Arthur Winter just when he least expects it. I belong in this town. And nobody, nobody, makes a fool of me. *(The music again erupts as he skates off into the wings. The lights return to Lindsay at the table. She is numbly fighting sleep and unaware that Johnny is on the landing, watching. When he speaks, she is startled.)*

JOHNNY. Jet lag?

LINDSAY. Huh? Oh. No. No. More like Beck lag.

JOHNNY. He made one of my favorite movies.

LINDSAY. Really?

JOHNNY. Yup. A thing called *Bikini Tops, Bikini Bottoms.* All the girls were flabby with blotchy skin. Five corpulent nymphets searching for a plot. It's a triumph. Mind if I join you?

LINDSAY. It's your house.

JOHNNY. Cottage.

LINDSAY. Cottage. Please do.

JOHNNY. I once owned three houses. Before I went to prison, I sold the other two. I don't miss them. How many houses do you own?

LINDSAY. None. I rent. I've got a one-and-a-half bedroom apartment in one of Santa Monica's lesser neighborhoods.

JOHNNY. You're very attractive.

LINDSAY. I don't feel very attractive.

JOHNNY. Yes, you do. You just say that because you've learned that modesty magnifies accomplishment.

LINDSAY. What accomplishment?

JOHNNY. I thought attractiveness was an accomplishment *a priori*. Kind of a Red Badge of West Coast Courage

LINDSAY. Are you going to write the screenplay?

JOHNNY. *(Enjoying her, laughs.)* "Her legs were long. Her heart was short."

LINDSAY. Or are you just going to jerk us around for a while, then send us home?

JOHNNY. To your unassuming little hovel in Santa Monica?

LINDSAY. Something like that.

JOHNNY. I presume Arthur sent you along to keep Nate from chewing the furniture. But no matter how hard you try, he still manages to embarrass.

LINDSAY. Something like that.

JOHNNY. I knew a producer once who ate like a starving jungle beast. At buffets, people would stagger back and watch in open-mouthed horror. He was a millionaire several times over; and yet, he had the table manners of a feral dog. How does Nate eat?

LINDSAY. I don't ... I mean, I haven't noticed.

JOHNNY. Oh, with this guy, you would have noticed. His chin was always glistening with animal fat. One Christmas, I gave him a bib.

LINDSAY. What'd he say?

JOHNNY. Nothing. He wanted my services. Insults were an inconvenience.

LINDSAY. You don't think much of us, do you?

JOHNNY. Us?

LINDSAY. Hollywood.

JOHNNY. Hollywood made me rich.

LINDSAY. And?

JOHNNY. Don't bite the hand that feeds you. *(A moment.)*

And if I don't write the screenplay?

LINDSAY. Golden Mirror will back out. You'll be left with Nate Beck scrambling from production company to production company.

JOHNNY. And if I do write it?

LINDSAY. We'll make a movie. *(Johnny smiles. This woman's directness is appealing.)*

JOHNNY. I never married. Do you know why?

LINDSAY. No.

JOHNNY. Because I'm a misogynistic prick.

LINDSAY. Is there any other kind?

JOHNNY. You're one of those unflappable industry women. I like that. You probably jog, have a private trainer, eat roughage for lunch, date CAA agents, sign contracts with a Montblanc, and caress the steering wheel of your Jaguar as if it were Tarzan's thigh. I bet if your *Daily Variety* doesn't arrive in the morning, you have the thing Fed Exed to your car. Am I right?

LINDSAY. I'm not even sure what roughage is.

JOHNNY. And at the end of a long day at the studio, you arrive home to your modest little apartment and you look around at your life and you confront that modest little Hollywood lie head-on. And it eats at you. It crawls under your translucent skin like some Third World parasite. You're beautiful and you're smart and you wear your position with astounding grace. But somehow, "Please, let there be something else. Let there be more. Please." And that's the lie. There is no more. You don't make movies. You make contacts. And you don't engage with the great minds. You sign checks at the great restaurants. And you don't sleep with the giants. You sleep alone. In a squalid little room in Santa Monica. Far from the madding crowd. *(A demonic smile.)* How am I doing so far?

LINDSAY. Arthur told me you relished these kinds of sordid mind games.

JOHNNY. Arthur was right. *(Long pause. Lindsay begins to walk about the room, almost as if stalking. Now it's her turn.)*

LINDSAY. Despite what you think, I'm not a studio concubine, Mr. Simmons. I'm here to try to get you to write a screenplay. That's my job. And it ain't pretty, but I drew the short straw. And, yes, I do jog. I do own a Montblanc. I do sign the check at great restaurants. I do panic if the trades don't arrive in the morning. And I do have parasites crawling beneath my translucent skin. But I'm not an industry whore. *(With contempt.)* "I'll do the screenplay if you give me the girl. An unconditional trade!" You are such a presumptuous jerk! *(Johnny laughs and applauds lightly. Relentless, she applauds back.)* And Nate, for once in his life, is right. This place is Gothic creepy. You probably have five million bucks buried under a rock somewhere and you live like.... *(Indicating the room.)* Like some shell-shocked loser.... Like this!

JOHNNY. My decorator died.

LINDSAY. No shit!

JOHNNY. Cara occasionally tries to "brighten it up." I admire her tenacity.

LINDSAY. Sisters are like that. *(A long moment. Johnny is taken off guard by her observation. He has begun to limp again.)*

JOHNNY. Do you have brothers?

LINDSAY. One.

JOHNNY. What's he like?

LINDSAY. I don't see him that much anymore.

JOHNNY. Estranged?

LINDSAY. Nope. Just geography and ...

JOHNNY. *(Suddenly looking down.)* Don't tell him about my leg. Mum's the word.

LINDSAY. Huh?

JOHNNY. My leg. I hear people talking. They like to joke about it.

LINDSAY. What people?

JOHNNY. *(Quickly.)* Who told you Cara was my sister?

LINDSAY. She told me. Why? Is it a secret?

JOHNNY. I knew a man once who had a maid named Gwendolyn. A Camelot of a name. A Cinderella of a girl. She worked feverishly from dawn 'til dusk. Never once did the man tell anybody she was his sister. He paid her poorly and never introduced her to friends. One day she died. Just died. They found her sprawled beneath the grand piano that she had been gold leafing for months. The brother was inconsolable. Good help is so hard to find. *(An admission.)* Cara thinks I'm crazy. *(Lindsay is disquieted. Now very on the edge, Johnny limps severely.)*

LINDSAY. She adores you.

JOHNNY. She thinks I'm crazy because of that night when Ron died. She thinks I snapped after that. She'd visit me in prison and she'd cry all the way home. She'd drive the miles and cry.

LINDSAY. Did she tell you that?

JOHNNY. I've always been able to sense the pain and sadness behind closed doors. It's my gift. My one extraordinary gift. *(The lights crossfade to the cherry orchard. The past. A fat moon sits low in the sky. Skeletal trees. The noises of night. Ron has wrapped himself in the* Winnie the Pooh *comforter. He still shivers. He looks up with wonder at the moon.)*

RON. "The moon is made of green cheese." Who came up with that? *(Johnny moves from the kitchen into the cherry orchard. He has the gun.)* It seems like this stupid cherry orchard has been here forever. You'd think it'd be condos by now. Minimalls. *(A moment.)* I never liked cherries. Cherry Cobbler. Cherry Pie. Cherry Ice Cream. They all taste like … cherries.

JOHNNY. Let's go back to the house.

RON. No, Johnny. Now is the time. Now is the perfect time.

JOHNNY. Please, Ron.

RON. I called Cara. You know, I thought she should know. *(Reflectively.)* Imagine marrying a guy named Cecil Meecel. What kind of a brain lapse is that? You like him?

JOHNNY. No.

RON. I felt hurt when I wasn't invited to the wedding. You know, really hurt. I mean, I should have been asked. Maybe not.

JOHNNY. Maybe not?

RON. I probably wouldn't have gone, but I should have been asked.

JOHNNY. What are you talking about? "Should have been asked." Where the hell's your mind?

RON. *(Years of anger erupting.)* Hey, don't pull that shit on me now! That I'm the big deal famous older brother and you're just this stupid landscape grass cutting moron! I've had it with that, Johnny! My whole fucking life I've had it with that!!

JOHNNY. Well, that's too damned bad, Ron! But maybe that's just the way the cards fell!

RON. You were lucky, Johnny!

JOHNNY. Lucky, my ass!

RON. Lucky! Big Deal Johnny Simmons! Big Deal Oscar Night Johnny Simmons! Big deal in his Big Deal Tuxedo Johnny Simmons with his arm around some Big Deal Film Babe Johnny Simmons and I'm sitting at home drinking beer and trying to figure out how to pay the fucking electric bill!!

JOHNNY. Pay it with your guts, like I did!

RON. Lucky!!

JOHNNY. Fuck you!!

RON. Lucky, Johnny!! And how come, how come, you got houses in London and LA and probably in Nome goddamn Alaska! And how come I was never invited to visit?! Never even invited!!

JOHNNY. Maybe because I was afraid you'd abuse the furniture! Like you've abused yourself and your ex-wife and your future and every other goddamn thing you ever touched!!

CARA. *(From Offstage.)* Johnny!! Johnny!! *(The men freeze, both breathing heavily. Desperate, Ron tries to give Johnny the paperback.)*

RON. Remember, Johnny. Over my body. Read it over my body.

JOHNNY. I can't! Jesus, Ron, I can't!

CARA. *(Offstage.)* Johnny!! Ron!!

RON. It's gotta be quick! I don't want her to see me like this!

JOHNNY. No!!

RON. Quick, Johnny! Now!

CARA. *(Offstage.)* Johnny!!

RON. Now!!

JOHNNY. No!!! *(Cara enters at the periphery of the orchard. She wears a waitress's white uniform. Out of breath, she stops. The men see her.)*

CARA. Stop! Jesus! Stop …

RON. Go away, Cara!

CARA. Johnny.... What are you doing?!
RON. This is between him and me! My brother and me!
CARA. You called me!!
RON. To say goodbye! Not to have you here! To say goodbye!
CARA. *(Coming closer.)* Put it down, Johnny. Put the gun down.
RON. Now, Johnny! Jesus! Now!!
JOHNNY. I can't!!
CARA. Put it down!!
RON. Over my body!! Read it over my body!! Please!! Now!!
CARA. *(And closer.)* Stop it, Johnny!!
RON. Shut up, Cara!!
CARA. Let him do it himself! Let him do it!! *(Ron pulls Johnny next to him on the ground. He grabs his leg in a vicelike grip.)*
RON. Please, Johnny ...
JOHNNY. My leg!!
RON. Now, older brother!!
CARA. Stop this!! Let him do it!!
RON. I can't, Cara!! I fucking can't!!
CARA. You can't do anything!! You never could!!
JOHNNY. My leg!! My leg, Ron!! *(Ron grabs Johnny's hand, wraps it around the gun and holds it to his head. Both men are trembling.)*
RON. Shut up, you bitch!! You fucked up my life!!
JOHNNY. My leg, Ron!! My leg!!!
RON. Don't try to fuck up my death!!
CARA. *(Rage erupting.)* Do it, Johnny!! Kill the bastard!! Just do it!!! *(Blackout. Then, a single reverberating gunshot. As the lights slowly return, the cherry orchard and the past are gone. As are Johnny and Lindsay. Nate and Eddie sit in the front seat of a battered pick-up. Eddie drives. Popular music* drones on the radio. A filmed country road fills the background: an old fashioned process shot.)*
NATE. Women!
EDDIE. You can say that again.
NATE. Crickets!

* See Special Note on Songs and Recordings on copyright page.

EDDIE. God's little chickens.
NATE. Screeching goddamn birds at six A.M.!
EDDIE. No doubt about it.
NATE. *(A scathing look.)* What? No doubt about what?!
EDDIE. Just making conversation.
NATE. I come down and Lindsay's gone. I'm all alone. Cara's out milking the cows or something. I go upstairs, knock on the door, and our hero opens it just a crack, like some agoraphobic poster child. I say, "Have you seen Lindsay?" "She's visiting me," he says. "Great," I say. "Can I speak to her for a second?" "Sure," he says. And he shuts the door! *(Astounded.)* He shuts the fucking door!
EDDIE. Jeepers! Just shut it, eh?
NATE. So I knock again. The door cracks open. "She doesn't want to see you this morning. She's taking a sabbatical from your rhinestone aesthetics." And then he shuts the door!
EDDIE. Typical Johnny.
NATE. "Rhinestone aesthetics ..." What is that? I mean, what is that!
EDDIE. *(After a moment.)* They probably jumped in the bog.
NATE. What?
EDDIE. They probably cracked open the oyster.
NATE. What?
EDDIE. They most likely shook the thistle.
NATE. What the hell are you talking about?
EDDIE. Sexual activity.
NATE. So why don't you just say it?
EDDIE. I did.
NATE. No, you didn't.
EDDIE. What do you think "shaking the thistle" is?
NATE. How the fuck do I know? *(Eddie shrugs, drives in silence.)* So tell me about Cara. Where does she fit into this nuts and berries asylum?
EDDIE. She's a peach.
NATE. *(After waiting.)* Thanks, Eddie. Too bad I didn't bring my tape recorder.
EDDIE. Cara used to be.... This is too weird.
NATE. What? What is too weird? What in God's name could

be too weird for this *Beverly Hillbillies* pastiche we got here already?

EDDIE. Cara used to be married to Ron, Johnny's brother. You know, the one he ... shot.

NATE. Cara was Johnny's sister-in-law?

EDDIE. Like I said. Kind of weird, huh? Jeepers! She tells people she's his sister, but she ain't. Like I said, too weird, huh?

NATE. I guess. I mean ... Jesus. I guess.

EDDIE. They never talk about it.

NATE. Was she married to the brother when Johnny...?

EDDIE. Nope. By that time, she was hitched to Cecil Meecel. *(Laughs.)* You oughta meet Cecil some time. Jeepers! He's a character.

NATE. Yeah. Right. Maybe we'll stay over. So where is this breakfast joint? I'll order the possum and grits.

EDDIE. They don't have grits.

NATE. *(A long look.)* You got family?

EDDIE. Nope. Never tied the bow.

NATE. The knot. Never tied the knot.

EDDIE. You neither?

NATE. I'm married. Was married ...

EDDIE. You just said you never tied the bow.

NATE. I said, "I never tied the knot."

EDDIE. How come?

NATE. How come what?

EDDIE. How come you never tied the bow? *(In an exaggerated gesture of despair, Nate buries his head in his hands and moans. The lights rapidly crossfade to Johnny's room. Lindsay is alone. Clearly exhausted, she looks out the one tiny window. Sunlight splinters in. Then, she starts for the door, tentatively looking back. Johnny enters from the bathroom, still in colorless gray clothing. She freezes, unsure of herself. Johnny is immutable.)*

LINDSAY. Nate's probably crazy by now. It doesn't take much to set him off. Then you're stuck with two hours of invective ... *(Nothing.)* I really have to go, Johnny. *(Trying levity.)* We've been here all night. You know, the Johnny Simmons Lecture Series ...

JOHNNY. Uh huh. So, do you feel like a slut?
LINDSAY. What? No. Of course not. Nothing happened, remember? You've just been ... reciting.
JOHNNY. Nothing?
LINDSAY. You started reciting *Mrs. Sedgewick's Head.* I started listening. And the moon went down and the sun came up and ...
JOHNNY. Nothing?
LINDSAY. *(Warily.)* Nothing. C'mon, Johnny. *(Johnny suddenly begins to pace. The limp gradually returns.)*
JOHNNY. I loved Ron. We had unique history together. We shared our pasts and our parents and our.... My little brother. *(Reliving it.)* He held on to my leg so hard. You've heard the expression, "Death Grip"? That's what he had me in. A death grip. And it doesn't go away. That desperate tightness. It lives there all the time waiting to erupt. And the pain ...
LINDSAY. Johnny, please ...
JOHNNY. And the pain.... The pain travels straight to my heart ... *(Laughs.)* Maybe I should have been a romance novelist, eh, Ms. McCall? *(Quickly.)* Did you read *Mrs. Sedgewick's Head?*
LINDSAY. Huh?
JOHNNY. I memorized it, you know.
LINDSAY. I know. You've been doing it for hours.
JOHNNY. What's the matter? Unfond of the author's purity of voice?
LINDSAY. Unfond of being a sounding board, yes. Unfond of not sleeping, traveling with Nate Lunatic Beck, being negotiated as if I were some singles bar trophy ...
JOHNNY. *(Not hearing.)* Walking back and forth in my cell, trapping the words as if my mind were a cage. I even memorized the things I cut out. Care to hear a rejected passage or two, Ms. McCall? *(Without hesitation, Johnny begins to recite an omitted sequence from* Mrs. Sedgewick's Head.*)*

"On the way home, Bobby and I sat mutely in the back seat. Mr. Sedgewick drove. Mrs. Sedgewick sat beside him. Her parabolic head obscured the night like some irregular land form. When they dropped me off, she said, 'Remember, honey, forget those itsy silly babies in those itsy silly jars!' *(A certain urgency.)*

"But I couldn't forget the babies. I had to tell my parents. I found them in the den. Ron had lost a tooth and they'd miraculously discovered it in the mouth of a tangled Howdy Doody marionette. My marionette! I started to talk about the carnival, but they were too preoccupied with Ron's ironies to bother with mine. They quickly put me to bed with perfunctory kisses and lingering adult laughter. As I tried to sleep, I could hear Ron's sweet rhythmic breathing in the bunk below. I was twelve. Ron was five. And that was the first time I planned to kill him. *(Lindsay is frozen, unnerved.)*

"Over the years, I plotted his death many times. And I plotted it that day when he came to my door, weak. Vulnerable. Familial prey. *(As if it were yesterday.)*

"'Mercy killing!' A phrase so deliciously oxymoronic as to tickle even the dullest of murderers. Indeed, Cain might have intoned it over the freshly bludgeoned Abel. Like a film in my brain, I could see the killing unfold inexorably. Scene by scene. Until finally, when opportunity came, with that opaque October chill in the air and with my heart exploding with terror and joy, I pulled the trigger. *(A whisper.)*

"Bang. And I felt his tepid blood upon my hands. And I saw the glaze in his dead eyes. Like the eyes of a fish in a monger's basket. Or a moose grotesquely pinioned to a lodge wall. Or the eyes of a baby in a carnival jar. *(A breath.)*

"Thank you, dear deformed Mrs. Sedgewick. You gave me the pain to write. And the power to murder. And write I must. And murder I have." *(A cold dull madness.)*

You are.

LINDSAY. *(Beyond wary, terrified.)* I am what?

JOHNNY. We all are. Hollywood sluts. Tramps in the Garden of Allah. *(As if a conclusion.)* I'll do the screenplay. A deal's a deal.

LINDSAY. Nothing happened!

JOHNNY. You all dropped me!

LINDSAY. Johnny, nothing...!

JOHNNY. As if I were dead! As if I were this interchangeable clot of sludge in the cesspool you people call The Industry!!

LINDSAY. Johnny...?!

JOHNNY. *(Violently, limping severely.)* I said I'd do the screenplay!! A deal's a deal's a deal's a deal's a deal!! *(Panicked, Lindsay rushes for the door and exits. Johnny literally collapses, clutching his leg.)* Jesus! The pain! Let me go, Ron!! The fucking pain!!! *(Blackout. And from the darkness: a desperate yell.)* Cara!! Cara!!! *(The lights sneak up on Arthur. He sits alone in a screening room. Light flickers against him. He is watching dailies. Pensive. From the booth, a Voice calls out.)*

VOICE. Phone call, Mr. Winter. It sounds ... urgent.

ARTHUR. Who is it?

VOICE. Lindsay McCall. She sounds upset. *(Arthur sits stone still. The film continues to flicker.)* Mr. Winter?

ARTHUR. No. I'm not in. Tell her I'm ... not in.

VOICE. She sounds pretty desperate ...

ARTHUR. I'm not in!! *(The lights crossfade from Arthur to Johnny's kitchen. Cara sits silently at the table. Johnny stands on the landing, lost. Nate enters, followed by Eddie. The two have been arguing.)*

NATE. Yeah?!

EDDIE. Yeah!

NATE. Yeah?!

EDDIE. Yeah!

NATE. Okay. The gloves are off! You chew like some cud-bearing thing. Some godforsaken animal thing with cloven hoofs. Like one of those South American cow things they always have at the fucking zoo. One of those lazy wide lumpy things that eats grass and pisses on its own hay. That's what you chew like!

EDDIE. Yeah?!

NATE. Yeah!

EDDIE. So! You left a tip!

NATE. Yeah? So what?!

EDDIE. You don't leave a tip at Jacqueline's Nook. Nobody leaves a tip at Jacqueline's Nook. It isn't done!

NATE. So fucking what!!

EDDIE. When in Rome, do Roman things!! *(Eddie stomps out. Lindsay appears on the landing. She has her luggage. She brushes past Johnny and heads for the front door.)*

NATE. Lindsay, what's happening?

LINDSAY. Get your stuff. I've called a cab. We're leaving.

NATE. Leaving? We're still waiting for a meeting …

LINDSAY. I said we're leaving. Get your goddamned stuff!! *(She exits. Nate looks to Cara. Nothing. He looks to Johnny.)*

NATE. What? What's going on?

JOHNNY. Better gather your things, Mr. Hollywood.

NATE. What'd you do to her?! What went on here?

JOHNNY. The lady is leaving.

NATE. *(To Cara.)* What the hell went on here! *(Cara is blank. Nate rushes to the front door and calls out.)* C'mon, Lindsay! We still have a meeting! *(There is no response. Nate comes back into the room. Impotent, he starts up the stairs.)* She won't talk. You won't talk. What the fuck went on here!! *(Crazed, Nate exits. Johnny comes down the stairs. He goes to the front door and closes it, never looking out. Cara remains seated. Silence. She and Johnny share a look. He starts for the stairs.)*

CARA. God, Johnny, I get lonely sometimes. *(Nakedly.)* I don't get lonely for sex or conversation or … you know, predictable stuff … I get lonely for somebody to just … touch the back of my hand or laugh at a funny face or care whether or not I get a haircut … *(She cannot continue. Johnny doesn't quite know what to do. Finally, he goes to her. He touches the back of her hand. She looks up. Embarrassed, he starts upstairs, dragging his foot as if it were a weight. At the landing, he turns on Cara.)*

JOHNNY. Every word. I remember every goddamn word! *(Johnny exits. Cara remains very still. The cab horn honks. Nate comes downstairs with his luggage.)*

NATE. So, anyway, thanks for the memories.

CARA. You're a crude man, Mr. Beck.

NATE. Yeah? And you're Miss Rural America. *(Leaving, stops.)* Just tell me one thing. How can you work for the man who killed your ex-husband? How the fuck can you do that?

CARA. He's my brother.

NATE. Brother-in-law.

CARA. Brother!

NATE. Brother-in ... *(Stops.)* Jesus ... *Chinatown.* That's what this place is. This big goddamn puzzle that nobody wants to make anymore because the average moviegoer is an illiterate fifteen-year-old with the attention span of a mayfly. You fucking people are living in *Chinatown. (The cab horn honks. Nate exits. Cara remains at the table as the lights cossfade to Cahill. He comes forward. His cast is gone.)*

CAHILL. *(To the audience.)* This whole Johnny Simmons affair has been a nightmare of twisted ethics and litigatory intrigues. No wonder Los Angeles has earthquakes. The Gods themselves shiver. *(A smile.)* Hollywood was invented by entrepreneurs, nurtured by moguls, and sustained by corporations. Yet, somehow, when "film" is the subject, people talk about Art. Even intelligent people. As if somehow Art were not a fortuitous accident. *(A final pause.)* Johnny is writing the screenplay to *Mrs. Sedgewick's Head.* I've negotiated an obscene contract. Johnny is again on top of the world. But his leg still aches. And he still lives in a dark room in a dark house in a dark town. *(The lights quickly crossfade to the restaurant. Lindsay sits alone at a table. Celebratory flowers and champagne. Music. Benjamin hovers. Arthur enters, approaches the table. He is initially playful. She emits a cold chill.)*

ARTHUR. Hi, Lindsay.

LINDSAY. Arthur.

ARTHUR. So, how was your vacation?

LINDSAY. Okay. I didn't do much.

ARTHUR. Good. You needed a break. Guys like Johnny Simmons take inordinate energy. You did a terrific job.

LINDSAY. We all got what we wanted, right?

ARTHUR. *(Uneasily.)* Right. *(Nate comes to the table, shaking hands with Arthur, kissing Lindsay. He is quite full of himself.)*

NATE. Sorry I'm late. I got hung up trying to corral this Encino dentist into a limited partnership thing I'm doing. Dentists! Jesus! When God gave out imagination, he did a dispensation on dental schools. No shit. *(Calling.)* Benjamin! *(Fawning.)* I can't believe it, Arthur. I never see you here. I thought this place'd be too *nouveau* for a guy like you.

ARTHUR. Why? Am I *oldveau?*

NATE. No. I just meant ...

ARTHUR. It's fine. *(Benjamin comes to the table.)*

BENJAMIN. Good afternoon, Mr. Beck. You people ready to order?

ARTHUR. No. Not quite.

NATE. How about some hors d'oeuvres? They bring a whole platter of stuff. They got "The Frugal Gourmet" tied and bound back there.

ARTHUR. Sure.

NATE. Lindsay?

LINDSAY. Great.

NATE. You heard the people, Benjamin. Some designer food and a bunch of forks.

BENJAMIN. Certainly. *(Benjamin exits. Nate looks around the room, waves. Arthur and Lindsay share a look.)*

NATE. So, Arthur, Cahill negotiated quite a contract for Johnny.

ARTHUR. Yes, he did.

NATE. He's a character, that Cahill. More moves than a Swiss clock.

ARTHUR. He's very good.

NATE. So what's with you, Lindsay? This your "quiet day"? Like Larry Hagman or somebody who says he doesn't talk one day a week. Christ, people everywhere are breathing sighs of relief ...

LINDSAY. Shut up, Nate.

NATE. Sorry. I didn't know we'd gotten so delicate.

ARTHUR. Nate, something has come up. *(Benjamin interrupts. He carries another round of drinks.)*

NATE. What's this? We ordered the hors d'oeuvres.

BENJAMIN. A gentleman at the bar, sir. *(Indicating.)* Mr. Andrich? *(Lincoln, dressed to the nines, stands at the bar and waves. They all acknowledge him. He exits.)*

NATE. *(Calling.)* Thanks, Lincoln! *(To the others.)* Do you believe this guy? Talk about balls. He must carry them around in a wheelbarrow.

LINDSAY. And yet another quaint little phrase from Captain Hollywood.

NATE. Hey, what is it with you?

ARTHUR. Nate, we have a problem.

NATE. We don't have a problem. Lindsay has the problem.

LINDSAY. Jesus ...

NATE. No, it's true. Ever since we visited that phony, all of a sudden she's got compassion and empathy and a bunch of other useless emotional crap.

LINDSAY. What phony are we talking about?

NATE. Johnny Simmons. That phony.

ARTHUR. Nate ...

LINDSAY. The man is not a phony.

NATE. No? What is he then?

LINDSAY. A pathetic shell of man. Mad as a hatter.

ARTHUR. Maybe.

LINDSAY. Maybe? Maybe!?

NATE. Face it, Lindsay. The Great Man conned you. He convinced you he was a basket case, then agreed to do the movie so that he could get in your pants ... *(Instantly, Lindsay throws her drink in Nate's face. Standing, she turns on both of them.)*

LINDSAY. *(To Arthur.)* Is that what you think?

ARTHUR. C'mon, Lindsay, sit down ...

LINDSAY. Is that what you think!

ARTHUR. It's ... possible ...

LINDSAY. Possible, my ass!

NATE. *(Wiping his face.)* Hey, you're making a scene here ...

LINDSAY. Fuck you, Nate!

ARTHUR. *(Standing.)* Lindsay, please ...

LINDSAY. *(Pushing him back down.)* Fuck you, Arthur! The two of you! You sit around like toy generals pretending you make movies and the people who really do it, the "talent," they're just conspicuous pawns. And every once in awhile you get lucky and it allows you to sustain your indulgent lifestyles. And so what if there are casualties. That's war, right?! Fuck you both! You privileged creeps!! *(She exits. A moment as Arthur and Nate sit silently. Finally, Nate cannot resist.)*

NATE. I like a feisty broad. What about you? *(Nothing.)* So, you said something has come up?
ARTHUR. Yes.
NATE. What? *(Nothing.)* You want to tell me?
ARTHUR. *(Getting up.)* I'd better go check on Lindsay.
NATE. Hey, Arthur, don't give me that "concern for the employees" bullshit. What's come up?
ARTHUR. I'll be right back.
NATE. She'll get over it. So what'd you want to tell me?
ARTHUR. You're pushing me, Nate.
NATE. So big fucking deal. I'm pushing you.
ARTHUR. *(Getting close.)* Fine. You want it. Fine. You're off the picture. Johnny Simmons won't do it if you're involved. Case closed.
NATE. What?!
ARTHUR. He says you insulted his sister.
NATE. His sister? It's his sister-in-law! Sister-in-law!
ARTHUR. Whatever.
NATE. This is a joke, right? Some convoluted Hollywood joke?
ARTHUR. No. No joke. Talk to Cahill. He'll inform you of the ugly details.
NATE. Off *Mrs. Sedgewick's Head?!* Bullshit! I own the option. You can't get me off the fucking picture!
ARTHUR. No? Talk to your lawyers. Talk to your agent. Talk to anybody. You and this project are history. It's done, Nate. Legally. You've been maneuvered into oblivion. You'll be reimbursed your option money and get a generous finders' fee, but other than that, you're gone. *(Almost sincerity.)* Sorry, Nate. Showbiz. *(Arthur exits. Nate sits frozen. Raw disbelief. Benjamin comes to the table. He has an overflowing platter of designer hors d'oeuvres. He places it down ceremoniously.)*
BENJAMIN. Your friends, Mr. Beck? Will they be back shortly?
NATE. Huh?
BENJAMIN. I've brought plates for your friends.
NATE. Oh.... Yeah. Sure. Sure. My friends. Sure ... *(Sensing*

the unease, Benjamin exits. Lincoln enters. He looks around, then cautiously sits.)

LINCOLN. Mind if I join you for a moment?

NATE. *(Still distracted.)* What? No. No.

LINCOLN. So what do you recommend?

NATE. *(A dull fact.)* Try the Mako. The shark fillet. They grill it. A little herb. A little butter. It's nice.

LINCOLN. I thought you said sharks eat teenagers.

NATE. They do. Who the fuck cares? *([Author's note: Ideally, this final sequence would appear on 16 mm. film. Indeed, as if a slice from the movie of* Mrs. Sedgewick's Head *were being screened, a coda using the actual participants as performers. However, if financial realities are prohibitive, the scene should be done as written, as it was in the original production.] The lights gently crossfade to the cherry orchard. It is the past. The moon. Nets of trees and a bright silvery light over everything. Johnny sits on the ground. Cradled in his arms is Ron. He is wrapped in the children's comforter. His body rests at one of those odd angles that only the dead find possible. Johnny is reading from his paperback book, although he obviously knows all the words. His voice does not waver. Beside him, on the ground, is the pistol. Cara stands beside him, still and very white in her waitress's uniform.)*

JOHNNY. *(Reading.)* "Summers were hotter then. And winters were all snow and sleds and cold anticipations. Poetry rhymed. And gas stations gave away free glasses. Yogi Berra leapt into Don Larsen's arms at the end of a truly perfect game. We hid under wooden desks, practicing to survive The Metallic Bomb. We had a milkman named Sam. And a barber named Clarence. We had paper routes. We owned ancient baseballs wrapped in electrical tape and coveted the plastic Chevrolets in cereal boxes. The Brinks robbers wore Halloween masks. Bob Cousy magically passed the ball behind his back. Our mother proudly owned a stone white Fridgedaire. And when we came home late at night, my brother and I would marvel as Dad's headlights would capture rabbits in their arc …" *(Very gently, he slides Ron to the ground. He stands, seemingly lost. Absently, he wipes his hand across the front of his shirt.*

When he removes it, he leaves a large blood stain, the only indication that Ron has been shot. And then, in an agonized whisper, he turns to Cara.) Jesus, God, the summers were hotter then. *(The moonlight abruptly fades. And then, a sudden explosion of light across the sky. It reveals Johnny and Ron and Cara in hot silhouette. Stars cascade.)*

BLACKOUT

THE END

PROPERTY LIST

Drinks (NATE, LINCOLN, LINDSAY, CARA, BENJAMIN)
Menus (NATE, LINCOLN)
2 octopus salads (BENJAMIN)
1 dinner salad (BENJAMIN)
2 dinner plates with food (BENJAMIN)
Silverware
Manuscript box (CAHILL)
Stack of mail (CARA)
Tabloid newspapers (EDDIE)
Toolbox with "Eddie" on outside (EDDIE)
Coffee pot with coffee (EDDIE)
Coffee cups (EDDIE, NATE, LINDSAY)
Package with pistol (RON)
Overnight luggage (NATE, LINDSAY)
Large, elaborately carved birdhouse (EDDIE)
Large, elaborately decorated birdhouse for martins (EDDIE)
Arm cast (CAHILL)
Papers (ARTHUR)
Cellular phone (CAHILL)
Telephone headphones (ARTHUR)
Magazine (CARA)
Instant coffee (LINDSAY)
Winnie the Pooh comforter (RON)
Paperback novel, distressed (RON, JOHNNY)
Flowers
Champagne
Platter of hors d'oeuvres (BENJAMIN)

SOUND EFFECTS

Nocturnal bird's screech
Airplane take-off
Airplane landing
Crickets, distant
Gunshot with reverberations
Taxi cab horn

TODAY'S HOTTEST NEW PLAYS

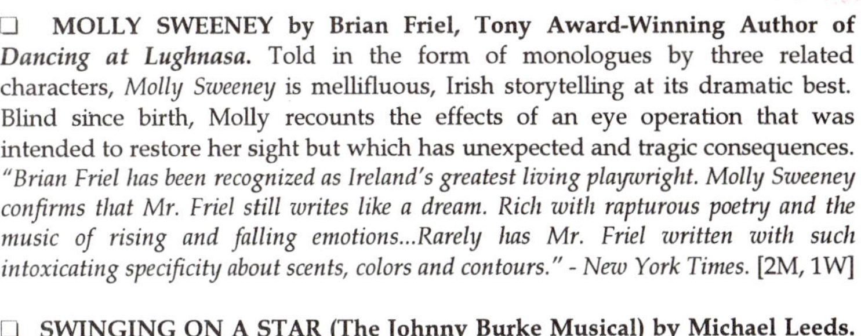

❑ **MOLLY SWEENEY by Brian Friel, Tony Award-Winning Author of *Dancing at Lughnasa*.** Told in the form of monologues by three related characters, *Molly Sweeney* is mellifluous, Irish storytelling at its dramatic best. Blind since birth, Molly recounts the effects of an eye operation that was intended to restore her sight but which has unexpected and tragic consequences. *"Brian Friel has been recognized as Ireland's greatest living playwright. Molly Sweeney confirms that Mr. Friel still writes like a dream. Rich with rapturous poetry and the music of rising and falling emotions...Rarely has Mr. Friel written with such intoxicating specificity about scents, colors and contours." - New York Times.* [2M, 1W]

❑ **SWINGING ON A STAR (The Johnny Burke Musical) by Michael Leeds. 1996 Tony Award Nominee for Best Musical.** The fabulous songs of Johnny Burke are perfectly represented here in a series of scenes jumping from a 1920s Chicago speakeasy to a World War II USO Show and on through the romantic high jinks of the Bob Hope/Bing Crosby "Road Movies." Musical numbers include such favorites as "Pennies from Heaven," "Misty," "Ain't It a Shame About Mame," "Like Someone in Love," and, of course, the Academy Award winning title song, "Swinging on a Star." *"A WINNER. YOU'LL HAVE A BALL!" - New York Post. "A dazzling, toe-tapping, finger-snapping delight!" - ABC Radio Network. "Johnny Burke wrote his songs with moonbeams!" - New York Times.* [3M, 4W]

❑ **THE MONOGAMIST by Christopher Kyle.** Infidelity and mid-life anxiety force a forty-something poet to reevaluate his 60s values in a late 80s world. *"THE BEST COMEDY OF THE SEASON. Trenchant, dark and jagged. Newcomer Christopher Kyle is a playwright whose social satire comes with a nasty, ripping edge - Molière by way of Joe Orton." - Variety. "By far the most stimulating playwright I've encountered in many a buffaloed moon." - New York Magazine. "Smart, funny, articulate and wisely touched with rue...the script radiates a bright, bold energy." - The Village Voice.* [2M, 3W]

❑ **DURANG/DURANG by Christopher Durang.** These cutting parodies of *The Glass Menagerie* and *A Lie of the Mind,* along with the other short plays in the collection, prove once and for all that Christopher Durang is our theater's unequivocal master of outrageous comedy. *"The fine art of parody has returned to theater in a production you can sink your teeth and mind into, while also laughing like an idiot." - New York Times. "If you need a break from serious drama, the place to go is Christopher Durang's silly, funny, over-the-top sketches." - TheatreWeek.* [3M, 4W, flexible casting]

TODAY'S HOTTEST NEW PLAYS

❑ **THREE VIEWINGS by Jeffrey Hatcher.** Three comic-dramatic monologues, set in a midwestern funeral parlor, interweave as they explore the ways we grieve, remember, and move on. *"Finally, what we have been waiting for: a new, true, idiosyncratic voice in the theater. And don't tell me you hate monologues; you can't hate them more than I do. But these are much more: windows into the deep of each speaker's fascinating, paradoxical, unique soul, and windows out into a gallery of surrounding people, into hilarious and horrific coincidences and conjunctions, into the whole dirty but irresistible business of living in this damnable but spellbinding place we presume to call the world." - New York Magazine.* [1M, 2W]

❑ **HAVING OUR SAY by Emily Mann.** The Delany Sisters' Bestselling Memoir is now one of Broadway's Best-Loved Plays! Having lived over one hundred years apiece, Bessie and Sadie Delany have plenty to say, and their story is not simply African-American history or women's history...it is our history as a nation. *"The most provocative and entertaining family play to reach Broadway in a long time." - New York Times. "Fascinating, marvelous, moving and forceful." - Associated Press.* [2W]

❑ **THE YOUNG MAN FROM ATLANTA Winner of the 1995 Pulitzer Prize. by Horton Foote.** An older couple attempts to recover from the suicide death of their only son, but the menacing truth of why he died, and what a certain Young Man from Atlanta had to do with it, keeps them from the peace they so desperately need. *"Foote ladles on character and period nuances with a density unparalleled in any living playwright." - NY Newsday.* [5M, 4W]

❑ **SIMPATICO by Sam Shepard.** Years ago, two men organized a horse racing scam. Now, years later, the plot backfires against the ringleader when his partner decides to come out of hiding. *"Mr. Shepard writing at his distinctive, savage best." - New York Times.* [3M, 3W]

❑ **MOONLIGHT by Harold Pinter.** The love-hate relationship between a dying man and his family is the subject of Harold Pinter's first full-length play since *Betrayal*. *"Pinter works the language as a master pianist works the keyboard." - New York Post.* [4M, 2W, 1G]

❑ **SYLVIA by A.R. Gurney.** This romantic comedy, the funniest to come along in years, tells the story of a twenty-two year old marriage on the rocks, and of Sylvia, the dog who turns it all around. *"A delicious and dizzy new comedy." - New York Times. "FETCHING! I hope it runs longer than Cats!" - New York Daily News.* [2M, 2W]